Willendorf's Legacy: The Sacred Body

Girl God Books

Edited by Trista Hendren,
Tamara Albanna
and Pat Daly

Cover Art by Kat Shaw

ISBN: 978-82-93725-11-4

www.thegirlgod.com

who have known Her in their personal story. All have spoken with Her and share something of their communion in this anthology.

On the Wings of Isis: Reclaiming the Sovereignty of Auset
For centuries, women have lived, fought and died for their equality, independence and sovereignty. Originally known as Auset, the Egyptian Goddess Isis reveals such a path. Unfurl your wings and join an array of strong women who have embodied the Goddess of Ten Thousand Names to celebrate their authentic selves.

Mentorship with Goddess: Growing Sacred Womanhood
A Sacred Woman reclaims herself as Goddess – a unique strand, frequency and incarnation of her – essential for the completion and wholeness of the spectrum of the collective Feminine. Our bodies are the gateway to recalling this truth. Mentorship with Goddess is a workbook – a year-long curriculum and programme – a rite of passage – especially useful for the transition into autonomous adulthood – the process of individuation - and then also for the menopause journey.

New Love: a reprogramming toolbox for undoing the knots
A powerful combination of emotional/spiritual techniques, art and inspiring words for women who wish to move away from patriarchal thought. *New Love* includes a mixture of compelling thoughts and suggestions for each day, along with a "toolbox" to help you change the parts of your life you want to heal.

My Name is Goddess of Willendorf
Today more than ever, the image of the Goddess of Willendorf is a relevant one. Women and girls are bombarded with Photoshopped images of an "ideal" body shape that is quite literally unattainable. Remembering Willendorf's powerful story reminds us of the beautiful abundance of the female body, with all of her hills and valleys, lush softness, and fertility. You don't want to miss this body-positive celebration of the Great Mother Goddess!

For recent writings and news of upcoming publications, join us on Patreon @girlgodbooks.

*For our Daughters, Granddaughters,
Sisters and Nieces.*

*And, for Ourselves—
and the beautiful Goddess bodies
we each inhabit.*

Photo by Tamara Albanna

"Our concept of god would be so different if all along, from the time of the Venus von Willendorf period of prehistory, roughly 30,000 B.C.E., to right now, we'd never swung around and done a 180 from worshipping the Goddess to just worshipping a god. Think of the sermons! The rituals! The ceremonies! Think of how much they would change if we were equally hearing from both sexes about what it's like to find god in the body."

-Meggan Watterson, *Mary Magdalene Revealed*

Table of Contents

The Fierce Feminine Isn't Afraidto Take up Space

Tamara Albanna

I was always on a diet, it seems.

Even as a child I was told not to eat too much—so I didn't, in front of people anyway. Food was scarce, so I comfort-ate wherever I could to cope with the abuse I suffered on a daily basis. This of course became the precursor to an eating disorder later on in life.

When I look at pictures of myself from 20 years ago, I can recall I was on a diet then too, despite the fact I was already so slim. It was around that time that someone close to me said, "I can't take you there looking like that!"

She was referring to going "home" to Baghdad to see extended family. I clearly wasn't in the best shape I could be in, despite being at my lowest weight as an adult. There was so much value put on my appearance—and most importantly the size of my waist—that I assumed everyone in Baghdad must be thin as rails for one reason or another. Of course, this was completely illogical, but the obsession to make oneself almost disappear in a patriarchal society didn't make sense to me until much later on.

They were trying to disappear me. Make me a pretty little inconspicuous thing—a non-threatening thing. One who took up no space, one who didn't speak. I thought this was normal.

Well, that was until I met my Grandmother and Aunts.

I saw fairly tall, well-built, but most importantly voluptuous women. Women with breasts, bellies, thighs and butts—women who looked like me. These women were colorful, loud, and confident. Their auras were incredible—they were a commanding, yet loving presence. A perfect example of the fierce feminine. I only wish I had come to this realization then; it would've saved me decades of grief.

It wasn't until I had my own children that I noticed my body start to change—parts that were soft before, only got softer. And even though this body literally sustained life, my children's and my own, I still fought it to death.

I would binge, then starve, then cry out of complete despair.

I saw myself as a failure, all because I couldn't maintain some unattainable ideal that society was ramming down my throat.

It was a battle that lasted for so many years—it was a part of me and my experience.

When I first saw the Willendorf, I was stunned. I had seen images of Earth Mother, and Gaia, with the large breast and bellies, but this image was different.

It was almost a sense of shock and relief at the same time.

Who created Her this way? Is She pregnant? Is She a representation of all that is—the Heavens and the Earth, all those who dwell here? Wouldn't it make sense that She be voluptuous— that She is soft?

She goes against all societal "norms" and expectations of how a woman "should" look. Perhaps because this was a matriarchal time, and women were honored and respected—their bodies, holy and life-giving.

The era of patriarchy sought to silence us, thin us. Disappear us.

I had to sit with myself and with Her for a long time. I had to allow this message to sink into my very soul.

The Goddess has taught me innumerable lessons—her many aspects and faces contain immense wisdom. But it was the Willendorf Goddess who held one of the most powerful lessons.

She taught me that self-acceptance was possible. Her message is evident even in her presence, like the presence of my Grandmother and Aunts. The fierce feminine that isn't afraid to take up space.

Let us listen to Her message, gaze upon Her incredible image, and remind ourselves to take up the space that we deserve.

About This Anthology

Trista Hendren

Willendorf's Legacy contains a variety of writing styles from women around the world. Various forms of English are included in this anthology and we chose to keep spellings of the writers' place of origin to honor/honour each individual's unique voice.

It was the expressed intent of the editors to not police standards of citation, transliteration and formatting. Contributors have determined which citation style, italicization policy and transliteration system to adopt in their pieces. The resulting diversity reflects the diversity of academic fields, genres and personal expressions represented by the authors.[1]

Mary Daly wrote long ago that, "Women have had the power of naming stolen from us."[2] The quest for our own naming, and our own language, is never-ending, and each of us attempts it differently.

The editors wish to note that Willendorf is known by a variety of titles. We chose not to police how contributors addressed Her. While many of us know Her as *Venus of Willendorf,* Max Dashu will share her extensive research on why the term *Venus* can be problematic. I prefer to call Her *Goddess of Willendorf*. But the fact

---

[1] This paragraph is borrowed and adapted with love from *A Jihad for Justice: Honoring the Work and Life of Amina Wadud*. Edited by Kecia Ali, Juliane Hammer and Laury Silvers.

[2] Daly, Mary. *Gyn/Ecology: The Metaethics of Radical Feminism*. Beacon Press, 1990.

remains that most people know Her by *Venus of Willendorf*—or sometimes *Woman of Willendorf* or *Grandmother Willendorf*. Contributors to the anthology have referred to Her by all of these names.

People often get caught up on whether we say *Goddess* or *Girl God* or *Divine Female* vs. *Divine Feminine*. Personally, I try to just listen to what the speaker is trying to say. The fact remains that few of us were privileged with a woman-affirming education—and we all have a lot of time to make up for. Let's all be gentle with each other through that process.

If you find that a particular writing doesn't sit well with you, please feel free to use the Al-Anon suggestion: "Take what you like, leave the rest!" That said, if there aren't at least several pieces that challenge you, we have not done our job here.

We struggled to find the right title for this book to convey what we were really after—which is the loving acceptance of our female bodies. More than that—our bodies are HOLY and a manifestation of Goddess. Kat Shaw literally was painting these thoughts into existence as we were sorting through all this—and Arlene Bailey came up with the title we had wrangled with almost the moment she saw it.

This is not (primarily) a historical book about Willendorf. Rather, it is about women and girls learning to love their Goddess bodies through Her powerful and timeless imagery. This anthology deals with the legacy of Willendorf. The cover art is not, as you will note, a literal depiction of Willendorf. We are all Her daughters. Her legacy belongs to all women—so She is not one color—or even that exact same shape—She is a composite of all of us.

Most books are years in the making. This one came together organically—and was magically pieced together within a few short months. Every time we browsed through the words and art, we became weepy-eyed. We knew we had found healing—for ourselves, and perhaps the world at large. May the body hatred of women stop everywhere. We are Holy. We are sacred. We are beautiful. We are the body of Goddess.

Centre
Jakki Moore

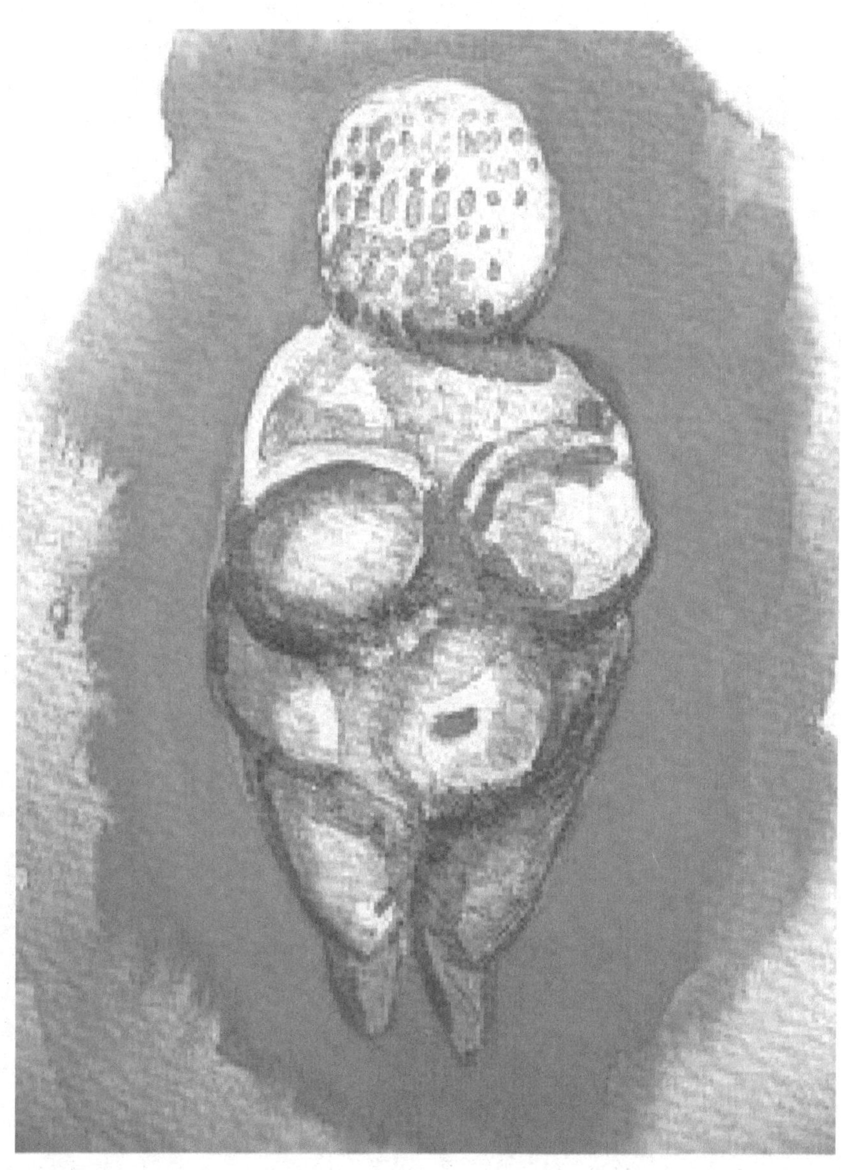

What's Wrong with Me?

Patricia Lynn Reilly

We frequent the therapist's office,

hoping the past holds an answer within it.

We fill the churches,

maybe god knows the answer.

We attend self-help meetings,

assuming an answer is encoded within the Twelve Steps.

We write "Dear Abby" and every other expert,

certain that they must know the answer.

We sit at the feet of spirituality gurus,

believing they will show us the way to an answer.

We buy every self-help book that hits the market,

confident that a new project will quiet the question.

We consent to outrageous measures

to guarantee our fertility or our attractability,

Convinced that the presence of a child

or lover in our arms will dissolve the question.

We sign up for diet clubs and plans and spas,

convinced that our bodies are at the core of the answer,

whatever it turns out to be.

We spend hundreds of dollars on new outfits to hide the question,

And on new body parts to eradicate the question.

And then at night after the day's search is over,
we binge on a quart of ice cream or a bottle of wine,
or we spend hours on the internet or phone
in tormented conversations trying to figure out
why the relationship isn't working,

Hoping that when we reach the bottom of the quart or bottle,
or the far reaches of the internet or conversation,
things will have shifted deep within us,
and we will know the answer and what to do about it.

Yet no matter what we do in search of an answer;
No matter how much we lose or how slimming the dress,
No matter how expensive or authoritative the expert,
No matter how many babies, relationships,
possessions we have or don't have,
No matter how spiritual, therapeutic, or recovered we become,
We are left with the same question over and over again
As we look into the mirror horrified
That the restructuring of our relationship, our womb,
Or our breasts did not quiet the question
There it is in the morning whispering from the mirror,
"What's wrong with me? What's wrong with me?"
A mantra that accompanies us the length of our days.

Originally published in *Be Full of Yourself! The Journey from Self-Criticism to Self-Celebration* in 1997.

Remembering The Old Ways

Patricia Lynn Reilly

There have always been women who remember the old ways.

Women who hold within them

the memory of a time

in the very beginning

when women were honored.

Women who refuse

to worship the gods,

to learn the language,

to take the names

of the fathers.

Women who refuse to twist

their female bodies out of shape

to fit into definitions,

to transcend limitations.

Women who love their bodies. Regardless.

Women who refuse to please others

by becoming smaller than they are.

Women who take space

with their thoughts and feelings,

their needs and desires,

their anger and their dreams.

Loud and strong
women from every age
wild women, spinster women
wise women, rebellious women
women who love women
midwives, witches
healers, activists.

Banners and placards aloft...

Eve, the Mother of All Living:
Take and eat of the good fruit of life. Take a big bite!

Sappho:
She Who Gives Birth Has Power over Life and Death

Mary Wollstonecraft:
Break the Silken Fetters

Sojourner Truth:
Ain't I a Woman!

Elizabeth Cady Stanton:
Whatever the Bible may be made to do in Hebrew and Greek
in plain English it does not exalt and dignify women.

Karen Horney:
Womb Envy is More Like It

Audre Lorde:
The Master's Tools Will Never Dismantle the Master's House

One by one the women step up
and commit the forbidden act
of biting into patriarchal thought

refuting it, smashing it,
discarding it and beginning again
in the very beginning when women
loved their bodies
named their gods
authored their lives
when women refused to surrender
except to life as it pulsated through them.
Women reminding us
there is nothing wrong
there never has been anything wrong
there never will be anything wrong with woman
that's why nothing ever works.
Stop asking the question!

They speak the truth of a woman's life
told with heart, mind, and body
refusing dissection
they are women and poets and theorists
who gather our brokenness
into their words
an impulse toward wholeness
awakens within us
and we become again
as we once were...
whole.

Originally published in *Be Full of Yourself!* in 1997.

Seven Archetypal Faces of the Feminine

Dr. Leonor Murciano-Luna

We are in "the time of planetary change… and transformation." One of the ways in which this is happening is through the conscious awakening of the Sacred Feminine within humanity. However, what we have related to the Feminine has been filtered through a prism of rejection and demonization, by the masculine paradigm of the Patriarchy. Thus, leaving us, especially women, with an unconscious disconnection of what the true Essence of the Feminine is… looks like… and feels like.

In my work with Conscious Feminine Medicine, the Feminine has been showing up in ways that honor the lost teachings and sacred power of the wisdom traditions. As I have incorporated the pre-daoist teachings of Dark Moon lineage – Wu Healers, ecstatic healers dating back to our pre-historic Great Mother time of at least 38,000 years ago… I find a web of new archetypal faces of the Feminine… coming through and making themselves known through this Feminine Spiritual Path of Conscious Feminine Medicine.

I realize that as a humanity, we need new ways to relate and embody the Feminine… within ourselves and our psyches, because the archetypes we relate to as the "Feminine" are either extremely distorted ideas of men and woman… or somewhat related to religious figures of Goddesses that are heavily dependent on masculine paradigms of birth, death and power. The Feminine itself has been lost… and we do not have healthy models in our psyche that hold the true essence and the power of Her, for us to integrate into our being.

In this time of Great Awakening, the alterations are happening in our mind and in our hearts, as well as in our wombs. We are learning to navigate through the portal of our hearts and wombs, which has been closed in the patriarchal survival culture of the last 5000-7000 years.

And as we awaken to the full portal of our hearts and wombs, we also become aware of how we have been closed off from these portals, navigating mostly from our minds, disconnected from our spiritual nature. We have been lost in the paradigm of mind, material and separation, operating with closed hearts and wombs.

As we return to our true sacred nature and realign ourselves with that which is life giving... life supporting and life affirming... we naturally become supported and loved from within, reconnecting with the source of life within. Awakening to the Feminine is also awakening to our unseen spiritual nature... as well as our access to Source on all levels. This is a marriage of form (body) and formlessness (spiritual Essence), a true union of our whole self.

Our divine reality is referred to as SHE. SHE is the source of life... that which we have turned our backs on. SHE is the source of love that we constantly look for outside of ourselves. We contain all the 'things' that we are looking for, 'out there', everything is contained in the spiritual dimension and sourced from the spiritual dimension that we are and we have access to, while being in physical form.

We are born from primordial Essence... that which we are calling Great Mother... God Mother... Source... Oneness... or SHE, that which is Infinite and Absolute. From HER... all else is sourced... and all else returns. SHE is the Great primordial Source of all... the Tao... the Infinite... the Eternal.

Patriarchal Collective

In our patriarchal culture we have lost consciousness of our Feminine Essence... and more importantly of our true spiritual nature, and in turn this has created a domination culture in which we look outside ourselves for our GOD (source). We have been severed from our source of sacredness... our source of safety... and our source of Infinite Love. In our disconnection, we have lived aimlessly... for thousands of years... trying to fulfill this deep void of separation focused on the outer world, the world of form. This is the internal wound we collectively carry, of 'thinking' we are separate from the Divine... because we have believed that story. This separation has caused much fear and an incessant search for fulfillment from sources outside ourselves. Our focus has been fixed externally... and there we continue to face the limitations, disappointments and disillusion of a world without heart... without love, without Source.

We have a lived in this domination culture for the last 5000-7000 years with an image of a father GOD... that does not give freely, does not create safety, and is essentially separate from our selves... our bodies and our hearts. This is a man-made image of Source... which controls humanity through fear and power, this is not the true Essence of Source, the Mother of All.

Another Reality...Orienting from a Loving Universe

Source is Infinite Love... infinite Joy... infinite peace... and many more sacred universal qualities which are sourced within our own being. "We" are the Great Consciousness that is Source... we are that in our individuated Essence... and manifested into form in this lifetime. We are the expression of the Divine... and as such... we ourselves are Sacred. There is nothing within HER creation, that is not sacred.

Resurrecting the Conscious Feminine Matrix

As we begin to resurrect the Feminine Matrix and embody this reality within us, we have to become familiar with HER... all over again and see the many manifestations of the Sacred Feminine that lay dormant within our DNA. SHE is within us... and SHE is that which we have called GOD... up until now. She is the one that gives birth to all of HER creation and is the quantum reality of all possibilities and all of creation. We must awaken to HER... and all of the ways that SHE operates within us... as we become awakened to our own sacredness and holiness. This recalibration of the Conscious Feminine Matrix is happening consciously, and unconsciously within our psyches. If we are conscious and open to this shift, we see the seeds of a new dawn... and it's new light being planted and growing within us... in this very moment... especially as the outer world moves through the chaotic transformation we are witnessing. If we say Yes to the Feminine within us, we become the ones that are anchoring and transmitting this light... and with it the new paradigm. This truth, HER truth is already within us... we are just awakening to it... and helping others awaken to it. We know it in our bones... it is written in our hearts and souls.

Seven Archetypal Faces of the Feminine

There are seven archetypal faces of the Feminine that have been coming through the work of Conscious Feminine Medicine... and want to be known and explored. But first let us clarify the Divine as

Source... as Feminine and as our primordial mother which all is birthed from. SHE has no other, SHE is also known as the Absolute, the Infinite and the all-encompassing. SHE is the Source from which all the Universal Qualities are derived from... pouring into all dimensions and worlds. SHE is the unknowable... that which always has been. SHE has been called by many names, most commonly known as GOD... the father, yet SHE has been the source of all inspirations, philosophies and religions. The primordial Essence comes through us and created us, in HER image. SHE is the stream of awakened consciousness that courses through us... and continues to awaken us to the seen and the unseen of HER ways. She is the magic, SHE is the Light and most importantly SHE is the Infinite LOVE that is always present, whether we see it or not. From HER womb, the ten thousand things are born. SHE is the Tao... SHE is All.

In particular, SHE manifests Universal Qualities of Light that are here described as archetypal faces of the Feminine. These living archetypes that manifest through us women, and all of humanity. Furthermore, these archetypes are a living field, separate only in our own minds and for the sake of the spoken word. As we awaken to the Feminine, we are able to consciously embody more and more of divine self... of Herself... within us. Awakening to these six archetypal faces of the Feminine allows HER to be born through us all.

Dark Mother

The Dark Mother is the transformative quality of life on this realm. On the physical plane, life is constantly transforming and dying... only to be reborn into another form. We see it in nature....

we see it in all material things. It is the process of death and rebirth. We, as women, experience it in our wombs, this monthly process of death and rebirth... of releasing and then preparing for possibility of life again, in our uterine lining. We experience these cycles of rebirth and death in our own lives... new stages of life always bring the end of something and the rebirth of something new. This transformative power of the Dark Mother, allows us to release the old to make room for the new... especially with our emotions and our narratives. The Dark Mother, brings us down into the underworld, where we can face our deepest fears and narratives of separation, in order for us to die to these false narratives, and allow our true light to emerge, being reborn over and over into our truth of greater Light. Yet the Dark... and these transformative powers of the Feminine have been demonized, feared, and made wrong. We fear the dark... we fear our own power that lies in our hidden fears and ultimately we fear death, because we have been disconnected from the eternal realm... and we see death as a finality rather than the transformative process of shifting paradigms that it is. Through the Dark Mother we transform, we die to the old... we evolve... and we have consistently give birth to new realities. This gives us the inherent ability to enter into the transformational alchemy of our soul... transmute our pain, and awaken to new levels of magic within us. When we stop fearing the 'dark' we begin to own the inherent power of transformation within us.

Ecstatic Feminine Essence

Our Ecstatic Feminine Essence archetype is really the embodiment of our blissful nature of primordial light. Within our being, we carry this Ecstatic Essence... it is who we are... it is our Light... the light of our Soul. This Ecstatic Essence that has been called our life force, is the very force of attraction in the Universe that desires to merge and becomes One. We carry this in our Essence and it is the origin of JOY and pleasure that we feel in our bodies.

Many times, we experience this our 'sexual energy', because of its blissful nature… but in reality our light is felt as a blissful ecstatic energy that promotes pleasure and joy. When we orient from our soul… we are able to tune in and feel our Ecstatic presence within us, acting as a barometer to determine what is in alignment with our Being. In other words, what is for our highest good, bypassing the intellect, and relying on direct experience and resonance. When we are in tune, with our Ecstatic Feminine, we are able to orient from Joy… and let Joy guide us, rather than orienting from our habituated trauma response pattern of fight or flight (FEAR), as so many of us have learned to do.

However, for women it hasn't' been safe to inhabit our bodies fully, because our bodies have been shamed and demonized, especially our sexuality and sensuality. So, we have either shut down our Ecstatic Essence, along with feelings of pleasure in our body, or we have opened ourselves up to acceptable uses of our Ecstatic Essence, in food and sex narratives. In order to orient from Joy and pleasure… we have to reclaim and re-calibrate our bodies to their natural state of Joy and pleasure, through the embodiment of our Ecstatic Feminine Essence and be willing to release the conditional responses of shame that have been indoctrinated into our cellular consciousness. We have to be willing to feel good about feeling 'pleasure' in our bodies… outside of the acceptable food and sex narratives. We have to let our natural sensuality lead… and free ourselves from the old dictums of being good... rather than feeling good. Embodying our Ecstatic Feminine Essence allows us to recognize that the Light of our Being is ecstatically blissful, sacred and holy, and we can source our ecstatic pleasure directly from within, independently of any outside sources.

Creatrix Feminine

This Archetypal Face of the Feminine is that ground from which all is birthed, as well as the continuing creative impulse that continuously births form into form. This is the creative energy of creation itself... which seeks to continue its birthing into something new, over and over again. When we embody this aspect of our Feminine Soul, we can feel the creative impulse deep within... inspiring us to continue to grow, evolve and give birth to something new. There is a deep resonance with life... knowing that life continues to express in a myriad of ways and forms, after death there is always rebirth. This is the creative force that is the birthing force related to the Dark Mother of death and rebirth. This is the impulse of life that promises to continue its evolution in a new creation, moment to moment... cycle after cycle.

We can see the manifestation of the Creatrix, in the rise and fall of the seasons and in Nature. She is visible in the first light of Winter, and the first shoot of Spring, in the full bloom of Summer and in the decay of the Fall. She is the creative principle behind all of life, and evident in the cycles of Nature. These cycles are also within our physical bodies... as the cellular growth and evolution are continuously underlining the processes inherent in our own bodies.

Creation continues onward as a continuous expression of the Divine. There are infinite possibilities of creation ready to inspire us and to manifest through us. When we open up to the Creatrix within us, we become inspired sources of creation, co-creating from the realm of 'all possibilities', whether we create projects, or babies, or find new ways to express ourselves. We each carry this Essence of Creatrix within, and its a matter of awakening to HER, and embracing all the ways in which you want to express your Creatrix force.

Cosmic Womb Mother

The Cosmic Womb Mother is the mother of all mothers and it is also the Mothering, nurturing template within us. All of human creation has been born through a woman's womb, therefore, the alchemical properties of creating and manifesting life as physical form is part of the inherent birthing transformational dynamic of the WOMB. The Womb is not just the physical matrix of the uterus organ... but the energetic aspect of the birthing manifesting Universal principle, we each carry.

Within the energetic Womb... the qualities of infinite compassion are weaved into the souls of each generation, anchoring our being with the Light of the Divine realms... while we navigate the often treacherous domain of duality. The light of compassion, union and infinite Love is anchored in each physical manifestation, whether we are able to creatively express those qualities or not.

The Cosmic Womb Mother impregnates us with the divine qualities, or the non-dual qualities... a bond so strong that it surpasses physical forms and lifetimes. A mother's love is known to be the strongest bond of all... because in reality it is the separation and creation of two bodies... from one. She carries the ability to deeply feel what is happening to her offspring... as if it were her own body... which essentially it is. This is the level of compassion... or union that is transmitted in the Cosmic Womb Mother archetype. The Mother's stream of compassion and union, is related to the Cosmic union of oneness... and as such it allows us to incarnate those non-ordinary levels of reality into physicality, through the matrix of our Womb.

Feminine Wisdom Keepers

The Feminine Wisdom Keepers archetype is directly connected to the field of Oneness where we can access the wisdom that has been held through the ages, without any limitation. The Feminine Wisdom Keepers is the archetype that holds this wisdom in place... and allows us to access this field through the portal inherent in this archetype.

Through the matrix of the Feminine Wisdom Keepers we are able to connect to our ancestors and to a time when we were consciously aware of the Great Mother in Neolithic 3000-10,000 BC and Paleolithic times. There is nothing ever lost because this field of wisdom is always available and it is through the Feminine Wisdom Keeper that we have direct access into this continuum of ancestral wisdom, collective wisdom, karmic and past life wisdom.

The Feminine Wisdom Keeper is able to access the information in between the world and come into union with the Universal Mind. Some call this field the Akashic records. The Feminine Wisdom Keeper keeps this portal open so that we have access to these realms from our physical embodied reality, accessible through the portal of our Sacral Womb.

Wild Woman

The Wild Woman archetype is the activating Yang force of our Essence. It is the life force that comes through wanting to interact... move... dance... express and communicate the active movement of Life itself. She moves... she expresses... she is full of life... and is completely moved by the inner impulses of Her life force.

She runs free like the wind... moves ecstatically in the movement... according to how the impulse is urging her to be. She is the powerful force of life within... and is also the vessel that allows the force of life to come through. She is not concerned with how it looks, or what others think... She is free to move and be in her wildness, in her joy, in her rawness.

The Wild woman only responds to the inner impulse of life... and takes direction from Her source. She is in tune with the cycles of the moon, dissolving in her inner cave during the dark moon, and howling, drumming and dancing when the moon is full. She is in tune with nature... with her Essence and with the wildness of her being, free from judgment and normative collective factors. She is the Wild woman.

Medicine Woman

The Medicine Woman, She is the one that knows that She carries the true Medicine for the aching hearts of this world. She is the physician of the soul... that is able to move in between the worlds and help others awaken, heal and reclaim their true Soul Essence embodiment while incarnated in our physical body.

The Medicine Woman of today... uses her spiritual gifts to help herself, her community and humanity discover and embody their spiritual dimension... thereby transforming their experience of living on this plane. She is aware that in her Essence... She carries, as does all of humanity, the Universal Qualities that heal the states of pain, suffering and separation. She is able to tune in and allow the healing of our heart... and the hearts of others... as She surrenders to the Innate Healer, directly anchored in Source.

Her medicine is one of consciousness... and she accesses these levels of consciousness in herself and others, through breath, sound, invocation and intention.

In the world, the Medicine Woman has access to the wisdom medicine of the Universe... and guides others, women and men, to fully embody their own personal sacred medicine. She recognizes that we all come in with varying spiritual gifts... ready to be manifested here in the world... and helping others manifest their fullest potential is part of her medicine.

The Medicine Woman knows that we are the Healers... we carry the medicine in our being... and it is our responsibility to discover and master our true nature of primordial Light... in order to heal ourselves, our planet... and manifest that reality physically. She knows that it is the Feminine, that restores the sacred truth of divinity within the world of form. And as such, She is the container for all the other divine Faces of the Feminine. She is the keeper of the Real Medicine.

Originally shared on consciousfemininemedicine.com.

Venus of Willendorf

Daniel Cox

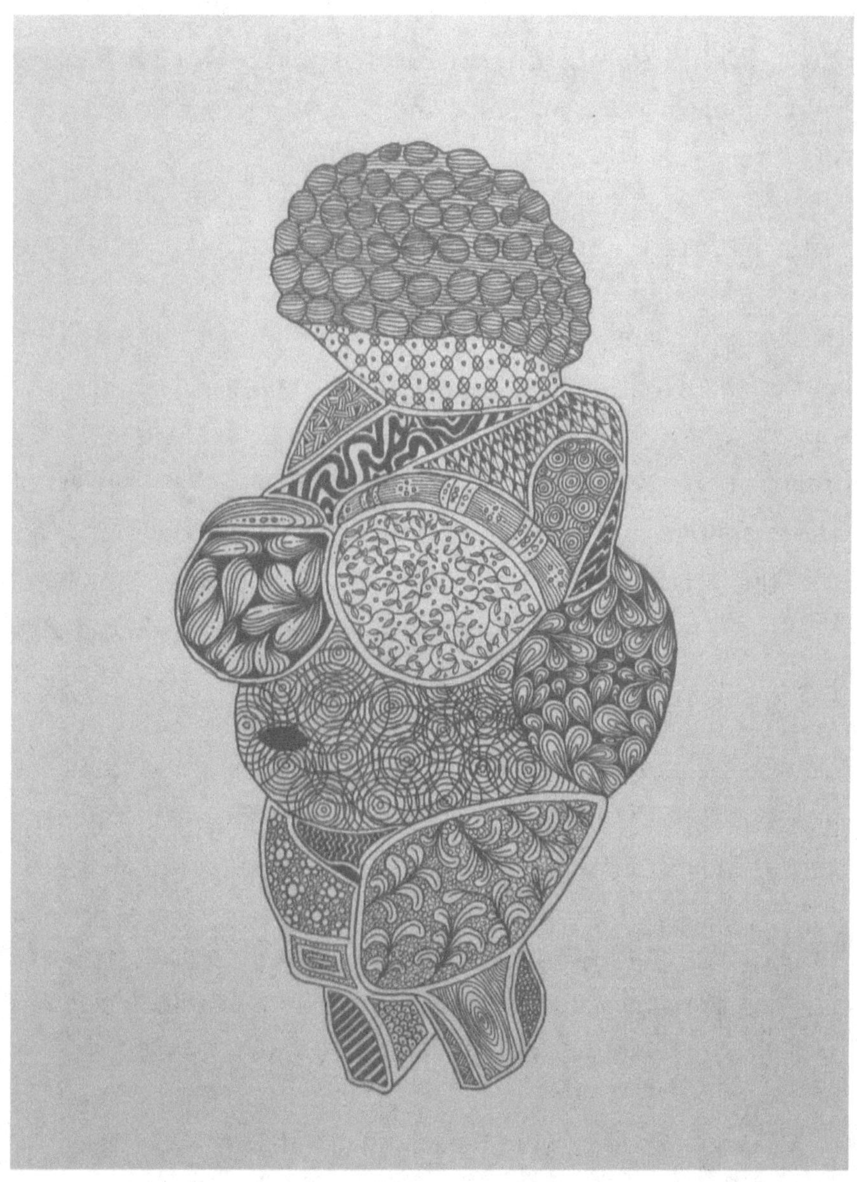

How I Have Expanded into My Fullness

Annie Matan

A year ago, I had a hard time passing a mirror without thinking harsh thoughts about my body. And now, I am proud to show her off.

I've come so far!

This week, a client asked me how I got to this point – where I am comfortable with all my voluptuous parts. We talked about white supremacy and patriarchy and how we are allowed to love our big breasts but not our big bellies. (Or bums or thighs.) We talked about how patriarchal societies literally buried the abundant Goddess icons that preceded them. (Listen to the *Mosaic* podcast with Carol P. Christ for more on imagining God as feminine and our egalitarian matriarchal history.)

We talked about the "health and beauty" industry that feeds and profits off the lie that we are inherently flawed and our bodies need constant adjustments, reshaping, trimming, lightening, hiding.

I shared that part of what got me here was a process of removing anything from my social media feeds that supports body shaming or diet culture and choosing to fill my feed with folx like:

- Sonya Renee Taylor, the Founder and Radical Executive Officer of The Body is Not An Apology.

- Adrienne Maree Brown, writer, facilitator and pleasure activist.
- Kelly Diels, Feminist Marketing Consultant.
- Angela Morris, Makeup Artist and Social Media Manager.
- Sarah Nicole, badass mama of 3.
- Peachy Keen Swim, body positive and ethical swimwear.
- Maron de Sade, Performance Artist.
- Neta J Rose, Actor and Multidisciplinary Artist.
- Christina Cleveland, Activist and Public Theologian.
- Trista Hendren, Creatrix of Girl God Books.
- Angela Yarber, Founder and Executive Director of Tehom Center.
- Aisle Period Products.
- Kathryn Hack, Artist, Mentor and Pastor.

...and so many more who share affirming words and images that remind me that all bodies (even mine!) are sacred and beautiful and normal and sexy and worthy of love.

AND I also take the time to hide (and report as offensive) any ads that encourage me to reshape, hide, or alter myself so I can feel more confident. I choose to feel confident in THIS body even as she hangs, bulges and droops in clothes that were designed for hangers and not humans. Instead of buying shapewear, I am investing in clothes that come in all sizes. That I feel good in. Sometimes they hug every curve and bulge so my expansiveness is plain to see. And sometimes they flow over me and slink around me in a playfulness that leaves more to the imagination.

I shared with my client that sometimes my daughter #GEM catches me doing curve appreciation dances in front of the mirror both on hard days and on happy days. And our bath and shower songs are the mikvah songs I learned in my training to become a Kohenet Hebrew Priestess at the Isabelle Freedman Jewish Retreat Center. Songs like *Reclaiming Inanna* (origin unknown), whose words are "I am a living temple of love. My body is the body of [Shechina] (the Goddess). Oh, I am that I am."

And then, I got to this point by having a #thisis40 photo shoot with Provocateur Images, with the goal of remembering my sexiness and desirability and then this new shoot, just over a year later, with Annie Caplan Photography, to reclaim all my parts.

And this past year, I chose lovers who explicitly, vocally appreciate my shape and fullness and who celebrate my curves with me. With whom I never need to hide or feel invisible.

And you. You all who have commented and supported and asked questions and shared your own stories. You have affirmed for me that sharing myself in this way is positive modelling. That #wearetheculturemakers (Kelly Diels). That my journey isn't just for me, it's for all of us.

And oh, it has been a journey. I have expanded into my fullness — physically and emotionally. From shame and self-judgement to joy and self-appreciation. I'm honestly marvelling at how far I have come.

So here I am. My own Shabbas queen. Celebrating sweetness, embracing joy, delighting in presence. Sharing my wholeness.

Photo credit: Annie Caplan Photography

Just as I Am

Trista Hendren

Just as I am, without a plea,
For I know my blood is H-O-L-Y.
And what's been stolen can be found,
O Goddess Willendorf now, I Am!

Just as I am, perfectly round,
Just like my mother's supple mound.
And every inch of me is lovely,
O rounded Goddess, She is me!

Just as I am, scorned and mocked,
for I never fit into that box.
Now love and tenderness I embrace,
O Goddess Willendorf, Here I Stand!

Just as I am, softer each year,
I hug myself to hold Her dear.
For all this lushness I despised,
O rounded Goddess, You feel good!

Just as I am, Thou wilt receive,
Wilt welcome, pardon, love, reprieve.
Because Thy beauty I now see,
O Goddess Willendorf, Blessed Be!

Author's note: This is my re-write of the classic hymn, written by Charlotte Elliott in 1835. As someone who grew up with these hymns, and still have many of them embedded in my heart, I have wanted for years to re-write them in a woman-affirming way. Singing these new words has been healing for me. We put out a book of re-written hymns entitled *Just as I am: Hymns Affirming the Divine Female* in 2023.

Bleeding Venus

Elizabeth Ogletree

Dear Willendorf

Arlene Bailey

These days I jokingly refer to myself as Willendorf
Standing naked in front of the mirror,
I see her in me, feeling her body as I feel mine
That ancient woman hand-sculpted from limestone
You know, the one ignorant male archeologists
labeled a fertility fetish with no value and left
to obscurity in dark, dank museum basements
As IF!

I dreamed of her once and she was so angry
So outraged at the insult that her body was ugly
Outraged that these idiot males thought
her body only for bearing children
Outraged that the body of a woman was
seen as disgusting – repulsive and useless
and definitely without sensuality or sexual desire
Outraged that some labeled her as the
Venus of Willendorf with the implication
she was nothing more than pornography in stone
instead of the powerful Goddess she was

I look in the mirror and see my body
My body that is daily becoming more
Willendorf-esq – what some would call
chubby and displeasing, but I see beauty
I see memories of a life well-lived

No children for me, but I feel my
soft protruding abdomen,
feel where my wombspace would be

And I feel Willendorf as her hands
embrace Me, hold Me, tell Me to love
my sagging breasts and generous thighs
I feel sensual as I caress my Yoni knowing
there is still plenty of pleasure to be had,
especially if it is only with myself, for no
instrument of patriarchy can understand
or appreciate the beauty of this ancient body

Immortalized in stone, one must wonder
how sacred this woman must have been?
How sacred to have been carved in honor
and held for all to see?

I see you Ancient Mother
In my mind's eye I run my fingers
across your body caressing your face,
each arm, your breasts and yoni, your
wombspace that birthed more than
you could ever imagine

Could you see as you were held sacrosanct
that one day there would be a world-wide
Circle of Women that honored and adored you?
Could you know there would be a movement
that would create life and ritual around the
myths and traditions of women from your time?

Did you envision that you would live immortally
enshrined in stone for all to see for thousands
of years and that one day women would hold
sculpted replicas and build statues of you?

That you would have women of my day rising,
defending who and what you were – all you could be –
to nascent male scholars bent on labeling you as
nothing more than a 'fat' woman whose only
purpose was to birth children or for male pleasure
or later to be the butt of jokes in academic circles?

Well my beloved Willendorf, I am only one of
thousands adoring and celebrating YOU!

For in this current time, there are many
feminist archeologists, anthropologists,
her-storians along with other scholars,
artists and authors who have shifted
the narrative of who you were and what
you represented. Truly we will never know
so we call you by many names and purposes
allowing for all you were to your people and
for all you are to the women of today.

For you, Willendorf, at least to me...

You are Woman and You are Goddess
You are Creatrix and Sacred Woman of the Earth
And it is to you Old One, Ancient Mother
That I bow.

Dear Willendorf by Arlene Bailey, ©2020

Earth Mother Magic

Pegi Eyers

You rise in my dreams,
like the power of stone,
breaking the glass door
between wind and the body.
-Patricia Monaghan[3]

Magic happens in amazing ways. We cannot predict the time or the place, or the shape of the mystery or deity that enters our world. As a practicing Animist, I have often experienced deeply personal messages and affinities out on the land, such as the appearance and timing of phenomena like a rainbow, the cawing of a raven, the patterns etched in sand, or the visitation of a snake. For me, having a deep companionship with wild nature is the very essence of animist knowing, and I continue to see, feel, sense, observe and communicate with other presences in Earth Community— creatures, beings, elements, plant allies and the archetypal animal spirits. I have also communed with inexplicable events and earth spirits in the landscape that are firmly connected to local Indigenous cosmologies. But until one beautiful warm summer day in 2011, awe-inspiring visitations from my Ancient European Ancestors were few and far between.

After a long hike through wild lands up from Stony Lake, Ontario, winding between dense forest, overgrown fields and outcroppings of rocky Canadian Shield, I was indulging in "earthing," which is the practice of resting on the ground for the regenerative benefits to one's body, mind and soul. As I casually looked up to the sky from

---

[3] Monaghan, Patricia. "Venus of Laussel." *Her Words.* Edited by Burleigh Muten. Shambhala; 1999.

my wilderness meadow at the clouds billowing overhead, they coalesced into the exact shape and archetypal configuration of the "Venus of Willendorf," the well-known carved-stone figurine from an ancient matriarchal culture in Old Europe. With stunned disbelief I watched as every detail became clearer and clearer, and SHE, this magnificent inexplicable feminine presence, hung in the sky for many minutes before hazily drifting off into other shapes and forms, as clouds always do.

Digital re-creation of the Venus of Willendorf floating in the clouds.

Humbled and shaken by this great visitation, to this day I am still learning to accept, and acquiesce to, the powerful consciousnesses that work through the natural world. Writing about this Great and Ancient Mother now, one of the primordial "Old Shes," I still can't discern the how or why of the Great Mystery, but hold this moment in my soul forever. I can see how human beings need to interpret and make associations with events that are unfathomable, to give our experiences individual purpose and meaning. What was my iconic "Venus" telling me? That every important cultural keystone connected to the land is stored forever in the body of the earth and the sky? That the spirits and ancestors will show themselves at the right time? That nature is a feminine force – ever loving and nurturing? That I am personally associated with cultures that honor the feminine? That the world right now has an urgent longing for the feminine? That I needed to recover the long-lost lifeways of my Ancestors, and find the trail that leads back to Her?

Found outside the Austrian village of Willendorf, this figurine is part of a wider neolithic tradition, and has been carbon-dated to 24,000 BCE. As modernists we can't know for certain if the culture included large, rounded women, or if the artifact was sacred or just an everyday object, or if it was exclusive to either women's or men's spirituality, or if it was portable, or part of a more extensive altar. Yet we can say with certainty that the neolithic ancestors of Old Europe held the procreative force of the feminine as sacred. The "Venus of Willendorf," if not an actual representation of a living woman, is an expression of fertility and all the cyclic earth-emergent chthonic powers of fecundity and feminine nurture. We can only speculate on the particulars of a culture that held these grounded values, but what a wonderful collective that must have been! Rooted in the truth of life, and the patterns of nature reflected in the human form, this beautiful hand-held object far transcended the female "beauty ideal" that was later promoted in the western world.

Red ochre had been applied to the carving, the ancient igneous pigment used worldwide to express the sanctity of feminine moonblood and the source of all life. To the ancient ones it was obvious that women, with their regenerative cycles, performed the same functions as the earth, which was the source of all nourishment, protection and procreative power.

Once established, a connection to Earth Mother Magic can never be broken, and the deeper meaning in my own personal mythology continues to unfold. Around a year after this visitation, I was blessed to receive my DNA profile from Oxford Ancestors, which placed my motherline 32,000 years ago among the ancient cave-painting cultures in the valleys of France. I discovered that I am a member of the largest and most resilient Celtic group, the mtDNA-based Helena Clan, one of the world clans descended from "Mitochondrial Eve" as traced by Bryan Sykes in The Seven Daughters of Eve. Without a doubt, at some point in ancient history my neolithic clanmothers either created the small "Divine Feminine" figurines that were found all over Europe, or were honored for their fecundity, fertility and wisdom in this way by the tribe. To explore this amazing connection through space and time to my life today, is an extremely thrilling ongoing project.

In the meantime, and as an affirmation of this exciting work, a dear friend arrived home from Europe last year with a gift in tow. From her extended holiday in France, she made a point of going on a day trip to Lascaux, to tour the beautiful natural landscape there and visit the replica cave and cultural centre. As I viewed her photos and listened to her thoughts on this sacred site so important to my own mythology, much to my astonishment she placed a Venus of Willendorf pendant in my hand, brought to me with care from my ancient neolithic homeland!

And to deepen the magic even further, my dear friend lives within a crow's flight from the exact same wilderness meadow near the shores of Stony Lake, where the Venus of Willendorf had appeared to me in 2011. Earth Mother Magic indeed! Honoring the life force in creation and knowing that all beings are sacred is the core belief of matriarchal, Indigenous and animist cultures, and it is our collective responsibility to support this interexistence with all life, with the highest respect and generosity of spirit.

REFERENCES

Norbert Aujoulat, *Lascaux: Movement, Space and Time*, Harry N. Abrams, 2005.

Max Dashú, *Icons of the Matrix,* www.suppressedhistories.net/articles/icons.html

Werner Herzog, *Cave of Forgotten Dreams,* eOne Films, 2011.

Burleigh Muten, Editor, *Her Words: An Anthology of Poetry About the Great Goddess*, Shambhala, 1999.

Bryan Sykes, *The Seven Daughters of Eve: The Science that Reveals Our Genetic Ancestry*, WW Norton, 2002.

What She Needed

Hollie Holden

Today I asked my body what she needed,
Which is a big deal
Considering my journey of
Not Really Asking That Much.

I thought she might need more water.
Or protein.
Or greens.
Or yoga.
Or supplements.
Or movement.

But as I stood in the shower
Reflecting on her stretch marks,
Her roundness where I would like flatness,
Her softness where I would like firmness,
All those conditioned wishes
That form a bundle of
Never-Quite-Right-Ness,
She whispered very gently:

Could you just love me like this?

My Name is Goddess of Willendorf

Arna Baartz

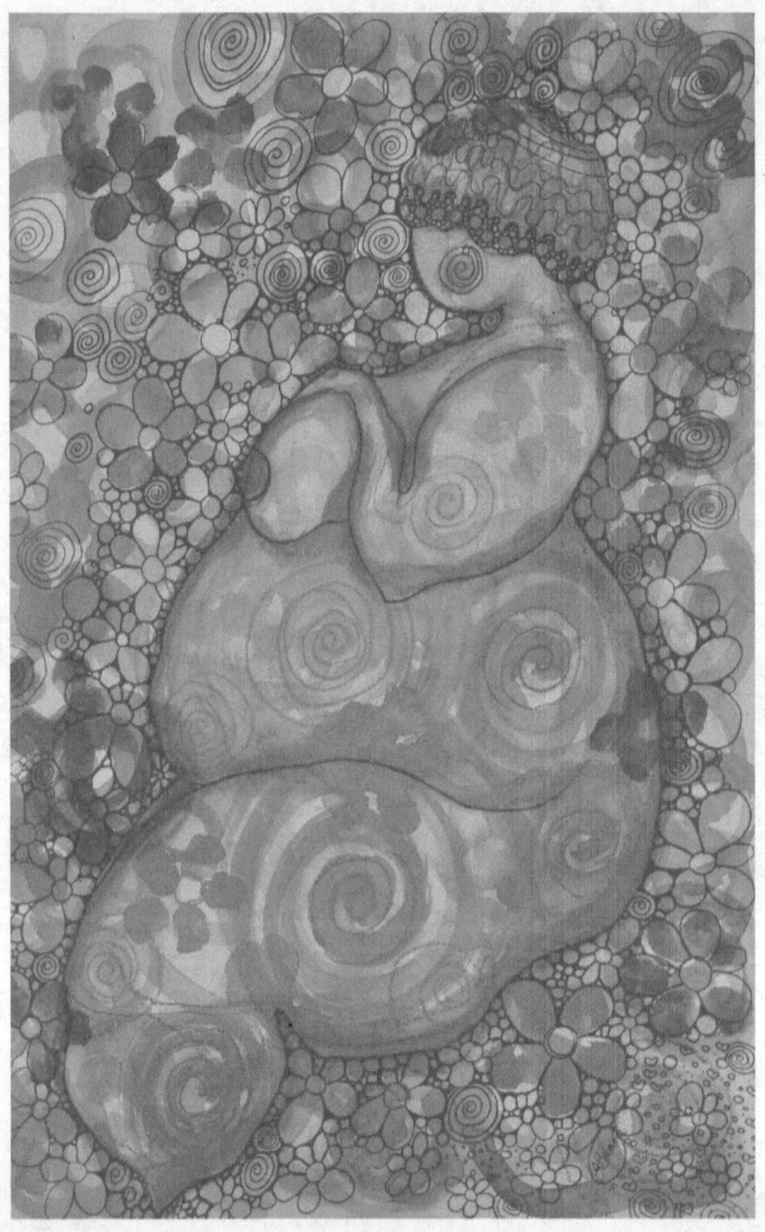

Illustration from *My Name is Goddess of Willendorf* by Tamara Albanna.

Does My Uterus Make Me Look Fat?

Molly Remer

"Loving, knowing, and respecting our bodies is a powerful and invincible act of rebellion in this society." -Inga Muscio

I do not remember the first time I ever saw her, but I do know that I have loved the Goddess of Willendorf sculpture for many years. When someone uses the phrase, "Great Goddess" or "Great Mother," she's the figure I see. To me, she honors the female form. I love her full-figure and the fact that she is not "perfect" or beautiful. I love that she is not pregnant[4] and what I like best is that she is complete unto herself. She is a complete form, not just a headless pregnant belly. She represents a deep, ancient power to me.

Ancient Goddess figures are commonly and frustratingly described as "fertility figures" or as pregnant, but most of the early sculptures do not actually appear pregnant to me, rather they are simply full-figured. One of the things I love about the Willendorf Goddess is her air of self-possession. She is complete unto herself. She may be a *fertile figure,* but she is not clearly pregnant and she does *not*

---

[4] There is some disagreement about whether or not the Willendorf Goddess is pregnant or not and many people do describe her as pregnant. However, I feel confident she is not intended to depict pregnancy. I have also learned that some people are so resistant to describing her as a "Goddess" that they will twist themselves into impossible knots trying to deny it. When this essay was first published at *Feminism and Religion* in 2015, I even received a comment from a reader who vehemently tried to convince me that the Willendorf Goddess had really been a "barmaid" who had cirrhosis of the liver which is what caused her rotund form.

have a baby in her arms, which indicates that her value was not exclusively in the maternal role. Early Goddess figurines are usually portrayed alone, it is only later that we see the addition of the baby figure at the mother's breast or in her arms. Logic would indicate that if ancient figures were indeed *fertility* figures, the presence of a *baby* would actually be more indicative of fertility than a large-breasted woman is, particularly since pregnancy itself, notably in ancient times, is not a guarantee of a live baby or of the generativity babies represent.

> *"...to associate the Goddess with 'fertility', and even 'earth mother', again limits the image of woman to a fertile mother – the creature the patriarchal male created, his baby-making machine. What's happening with all these descriptions is that the Goddess is being limited to areas where women, in the patriarchal male-seed era, were confined. There seems to be a patriarchal veil of prejudice preventing the Goddesses being seen as the source of wisdom, magic, fate, inspiration, change and spirituality – none of which need have anything to do with having babies, or making plants grow. Yes, women have babies, but that's not all they do, or are."* –Julia Stonehouse, *Father's Seed, Mother's Sorrow*

The earliest known Goddess figures are independent of specifically *maternal* imagery; it is only later that we begin to see Goddess defined in relationship to children or as exclusively maternal. I think this reflects a shift that women continue to struggle with today, in Goddess religion as well as personal life, with the mother role seen as exhaustive or exclusive. In contemporary society, the only mainstream representation of the Goddess that manages to survive under public recognition is the Madonna and Child—and here, not only has Goddess been completely subsumed by her offspring, She is no longer even recognized as truly divine.

The Willendorf Goddess has been a potent affirmation for me many times in my life. One Mother's Day, my then four-year-old son found a little green aventurine Goddess of Willendorf at a local rock shop: "We have GOT to get this for Mom!" he told my husband and they surprised me with it that afternoon. It still makes me get a little teary to look at it, because it was such a beautiful moment of feeling *seen* and acknowledged by my little child. When I found out I was pregnant for the third time, my husband surprised me with a beautiful Goddess of Willendorf pendant. I was holding onto that pendant during the ultrasound that told us that our third son no longer had a heartbeat. During my labor with my little non-living baby, I wore and held onto the pendant. It went with me to the emergency room and I could feel the solid, reassuring weight of her against my chest when dressed in a hospital gown, IV fluids moving into my arm, while blood continued to spill from me as my body said goodbye to my baby. I buried a Goddess of Willendorf bead with my baby's body and put a matching one on his memorial necklace.

On Mother's Day the following year, right after finding out I was pregnant with my rainbow baby girl, my husband gave me a beautiful new Goddess of Willendorf ring. I was little scared to wear it, because what if the ring too, became a sad reminder of a pregnancy lost, but wear it I did—up to and through the moment when I caught my sweet little *living* girl in my own grateful, be-ringed hands.

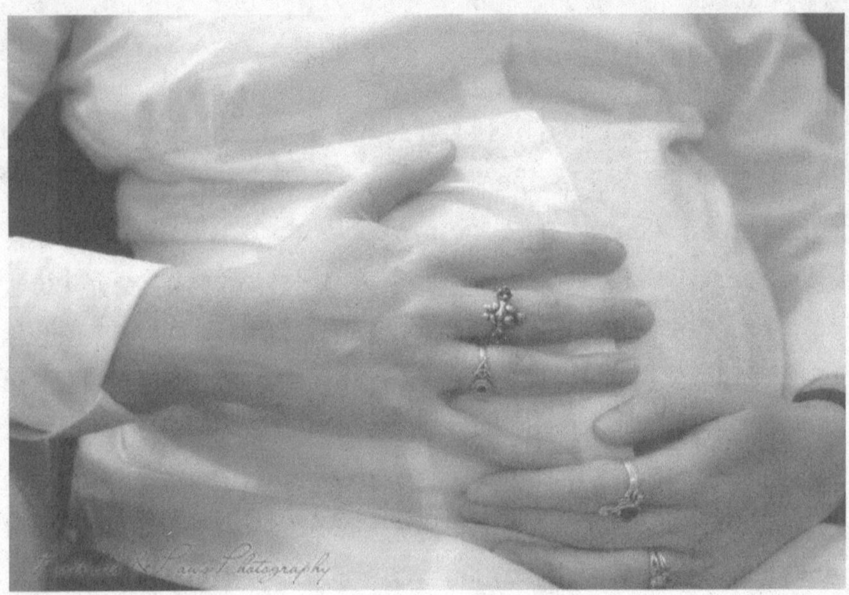

The website from which the ring was purchased disappeared— and I didn't see another ring like it until when I was on the phone making a wholesale order from Wellstone Jewelry requesting one of their Venus of Lespugue pendants. The woman on the phone told me, "We don't sell very many of those. She seems to make people uncomfortable. In fact, we used to make a ring too. A Venus of Willendorf ring, but no one ever wanted her. I think because she is 'too fat' and she makes people feel weird." Oh my goodness, I replied, I think I have one of your rings! I emailed her a picture of my hand and sure enough, though discontinued, I'd coincidentally gotten one of the last of the rings ever made.

What does this have to do with my uterus making me look fat? Well, I've had the experience of wearing my ring and having another woman, a wonderful, peaceful, gifted, gentle healer of a woman, *laugh at it*, like it was a joke ring. My mom sold a pottery sculpture version of the Willendorf to a man at a class and he laughed at this wonderful image as well, saying, "this is *hilarious*." Hilarious? Why? Because she is fat? Or, is it something else?

Several years ago, I read a post online titled *Does My Uterus Make Me Look Fat?* and I thought of my beloved Goddess of Willendorf, She of the Ample Uterus. While I can no longer locate the article itself, I remember the mention that even pre-teen girls have a slight swell to their bellies. The author of the post essentially said, "*duh, a completely flat belly IS NEVER POSSIBLE. THERE IS A UTERUS IN THERE.*" When I read it, I thought about women not liking the Goddess of Willendorf ring because she is "too fat." And, I thought of a couple of quotes I saved from the Our Bodies edition of *Sage Woman magazine* (Spring, 1996):

> "...so it has been: women's power has declined as woman's belly has been violated and shamed... 5,000 years of patriarchal culture has degraded belly, body, woman, the sacred feminine, the soul, the feminine sensibility in both women and men, native peoples, and nature—all in a single process of devaluation. Because our belly is the bodily site of feminine sensibility, our patriarchal culture marks the belly as a target of assault, through rape, unnecessary hysterectomies and Cesarians [sic], reproductive technology, legal restrictions on women's authority in pregnancy and childbirth, and belly-belittling fashions,

exercise regimens, and diet schemes... a culture that literally **hates women's guts**..."

–Lisa Sarasohn, The Goddess Ungirdled

And:

"Our bodies are vessels of the sacred, not the homes of sinful urges. Our bodies create and sustain the sacred. And that sacredness does not equate with any artificial notion of bodily perfection. All of us are fit habitations for the divine, no matter what the diet doctors, fitness gurus, health food fanatics, New Age healers, and the fashion police try to force on us. If we don't take our bodies into account in our expression of [our religion], then it becomes a mere shadow of itself. When we are fully present in our bodies [women's religion] becomes a three-dimensional, vibrant, fully fleshed-out expression of the divine..."

–DeAnna Alba in How to Flesh Our Your Magick

Even though I am a Goddess sculptor myself, it took me many attempts to make a version of the Goddess of Willendorf that satisfied me. I tried polymer clay, I tried pottery clay, I tried making my husband make one for me. None of them were *right*. Finally, my husband said, "Why don't you just make one using your own style?" This was the epiphany I needed and it *worked!* I successfully used the same technique and structure I use for all of my sculptures, but with a Willendorf-twist and I finally made a figure I was proud of. My husband made a mold from my sculpt and cast her in pewter and I wear her as a pendant when I need to feel powerful and confident. Her uterus might make her look fat, but to me, she is one of the most powerfully affirming images of womanhood I have ever encountered and there is nothing funny about her.

"Your body is your own. This may seem obvious. But to inhabit your physical self fully, with no apology, is a true act of power."

–Camille Maurine (*Meditation Secrets for Women*)

Appear

Fig Ally

She thought she'd exercise till her all was right
Saturate her cells out of their fright

Jump up before the moon had finished serenading the night

Lap miles
Calculate how much less of her she could present
to each new date on her calendar
As if the pages would hesitate to pencil her in
if her softness was still hers

She thought she'd close the gate
on anything she was so love could find her standing thin

Disappearing the disappointed mirror that secretly loved her all
along

The Venus of Willendorf Project

Brenda Oelbaum

I have collected a lot of things in my life—1930s pottery mixing bowls and tea pots, Fenton glass shoes for my sister-in-law, and sterling silver napkin rings with my family monograms and those of our friends for gifting. But one collection that started rather unintentionally did not really bring the same joy as the items listed above or provide the thrill of hours spent at antique malls, collectible shows, and yard sales. It would be from this bizarre collection that the Venus of Willendorf Project would evolve.

This superfluous collection started with the collecting of pounds and pounds of fat, a most frightening thing to collect for a preteen girl in this society. But the collection of pounds was only the precursor to the collection to which I refer. It was the collection of diet books that found their way to my bookcase. My attempts to turn myself into someone else haunts me to this day. Every few years I would come to my senses and throw them all out, take them to a used bookstore for resale, or donate them to charity, determined not to waste another moment of my life on the hopeless pursuit of thinness. And then somehow, years later I was doing it again, unloading shelves and shelves of diet books. If I had thought of this project years ago, I would have had a massive lead on my current creation. I believe I have purged myself of diet books at least four times in my life (the same number of times in a year I often gained and lost 50 lbs.). Shocking and an incredible waste!

Disordered eating, chronic dieting, binging, and overweight have been a dominant part of my life. Whether I was waiting to see a certain number on the scale before doing something, or wasting my life hiding and stuffing my feelings, issues of diet and weight loss have dominated my existence. This was evidenced by the ever-growing number of diet books that would find themselves on my bookshelves year after year. They never worked once I tired of the gimmick or unique way of eating. I would go back to my old ways and gain the weight back and then some. In fact, I am pretty darn sure they made me the truly fat person I am today. After years of dieting, I developed some awfully bad habits, and some crazy food rules, all of which contributed to making it exceedingly difficult to eat in a natural, healthy manner. I was so busy following some nonsensical food rules I had found in diet books or fashion magazines, that I was no longer able to recognize my own body's natural cues of hunger and fullness. I ate so much of certain foods that to this day I cannot even look at them in the market. Unfortunately, many of these foods were so-called healthy foods—fruits for example, pineapples to be exact. I can't stand the smell of ripe pineapple to this day because of the months I spent on Judy Mazel's Beverly Hills Diet.[5]

If you are not aware of this infamous diet, the first week was basically a week of eating nothing but fruit—pineapple, papayas,

---

[5] My mother likes to tell people that the reason I moved out of the house in 1981, at the age of 20, was because I wanted to live like a slob, not pick up after myself. The real reason, however, was so that I could do what I wanted to do with food. Judy Mazel's book came out that year, and I remember very clearly her diet being the first thing I did when I had my own apartment. If I wanted to eat nothing but fruit for weeks, that would be all that was in the house. I was doing the shopping and I could restrict the groceries to the diet of the day; whether I was binging or fasting I was safe alone in my own little world.

mangos, watermelon, and grapes. On the watermelon day, my stool (if I might be so crude) was bright red. It has taken me nearly 45 years to be able to eat a simple handful of grapes. You see, grapes, like watermelon, were only to be eaten alone, and if you started a day with grapes you could eat nothing else because the food would get trapped and ferment in your stomach and slow down digestion. My experience on the Beverly Hills Diet was training for bulimia; eat all the pineapple you want in one day and it just shoots out of you like a goose.

My favorite form of dieting was fasting; I could go for weeks eating nearly nothing. This created the habit of skipping meals and would often end in a series of binges. I know there are papers published in medical journals that both dispute and support my findings, but I do not much care what they have to say. This is my experience and until you have walked a mile in my shoes you can't tell me otherwise. It was from this painful life experience that the Venus of Willendorf Project arose.

The formation of the Feminist Art Project at Rutgers University in the summer of 2005 allowed me to revisit a more intimate and personal kind of art. For years I had thought my art trite – "Who cares about me, my angst and my depression? The art that really excites people is political, historic, and universal." Unless you are Frida Kahlo, you are not going to get away with painting only self-portraits, and so I stopped doing art about me and started doing art that was political.

While attending the 25th anniversary of ArtTable in the spring of 2005 I met a wonderful artist and curator named Carol Cole, and she was the first person to tell me about a project called "A Year of Feminism in Art" and that if I was interested in curating shows myself, I should think about projects related to this theme. Through this network I met one of the founding women of the program at Rutgers, Ferris Olin. At the time she was trying to make contacts across the country to create The Women Artists Archives National Directory (WAAND) at Rutgers. As it turned out, Olin was one of the major players of the year's "Year of Feminism in Art." It was called The Feminist Art Project (TFAP). As I sent her information, I received from the Michigan area, Olin came to invite me to be Michigan regional representative for TFAP as a whole.[6]

It was only after this invitation that I began to look at the work I was doing and remembered the old feminist axiom that "the personal is political." I decided to reconsider my earlier decision to stop making art about my own life experience.

The Venus of Willendorf installation is both political and personal. Every day the increasing government involvement in monitoring our food intake and dietary choices makes it so. In 2008, Mississippi House Bill No. 282 was introduced by Representatives Mayhall, Read, and Shows. Basically the bill would allow food establishments the right to refuse service to any person who could be considered obese. Even then-Vice President of PETA, Bruce Friedrich, speaking for the more than 1.8 million members and supporters of the organization, had to chime in regarding this bill.[7] In a letter dated February 5, 2008, Friedrich suggested the bill be changed to have the

---

[6] Little did they know in 2005 that the activities of the 2006–2007 Feminist Art Project would grow to its current importance. The TFAP calendar now goes as far into the future as 2023. Post-feminism? I think not!

[7] House Bill No. 282, 2008 Regular Session,
http://billstatus.ls.state.ms.us/documents/2008/pdf/HB/0200-

restaurants serve the fat people only vegan food. Yeah, right! Vegan KFC! The writers of this bill claim that they knew it would never pass, but they hoped it would bring attention to the "obesity crisis," like it needs more.

Then there was the Cupcake Crackdown. Parents in the state of Texas lobbied to get a "Safe Cupcake Amendment" added to the state's nutritional policy to ensure that they could continue to bring the frosted treats to school celebrations. In reaction to the federal law requiring every school system in the National School Lunch and School Breakfast programs to write a "wellness policy" by July 2006, some schools went so far as to ban sweets like cupcakes from being brought to the schools for events such as birthdays.

In 2004, after losing 110 pounds because of a diagnosis of type 2 diabetes, then-governor of Arkansas, Mike Huckabee, pushed for a law requiring schools to measure students each year and report to their parents whether pupils were overweight or at risk of becoming overweight. By February of 2007, seven states were on board with these Obesity Report Cards. Kids in kindergarten, children as young as five years of age, were being paraded into school nurses' offices for regular weigh-ins. It was not enough that we do this to ourselves. Now it was legislated and pushed on our babies. (Since Huckabee left the Governor's office in 2007 the BMI Report Cards have become optional in Arkansas, much to his chagrin) Though I applauded Mr. Huckabee on his original personal health success, he has over the years proven to represent most people who diet and regain the weight. I do not believe humiliating young children and creating a fear of fat at such a young age is

---

0299/HB0282IN.pdf (accessed March 11, 2008). For news about the bill, try a Yahoo! search for the keywords Mississippi house bill no. 282.

useful. Studies have shown that when mothers worry about their children's weight the children are at higher risk of becoming overweight.[8] Dr. Donna Spruijt-Metz, of the University of Southern California in Alhambra, points out:

> "When mother interferes with the child's ability to regulate his or her own energy intake, kids might lose their ability to self-regulate. In other words, they stop functioning on inner cues like 'I feel full' or 'I feel hungry' and start operating on social cues like 'time to pork out on chips because mom isn't watching' or 'there is no way I am going to eat this just because mom wants me to."[9]

Former U.S. Surgeon General Richard Carmona declared: "As we look to the future and where childhood obesity will be in 20 years… it is every bit as threatening to us as is the terrorist threat we face today. It is the threat from within."[10] Declaring war on the obesity epidemic! (It's hard to keep track of all our "wars.") The government should keep its eyes on its own plate; it should be managing the country. As with the abortion issue, it should not be telling us what to do with our bodies. This is obscene and guaranteed to make

---

[8] William C. Heird, "Parental Feeding Behavior and Children's Fat Mass, American Journal of Clinical Nutrition 75 (2002): 451-452, http://www.ajcn.org/cgi/content/full/75/3/451 (accessed March 11, 2008). Comment on Donna Spruijt-Metz, et al., "Relation Between Mothers' Child-Feeding Practices and Children's Adiposity," American Journal of Clinical Nutrition 75 (2002): 581-586, http://www.ajcn.org/cgi/content/full/75/3/581 (accessed March 11, 2008).

[9] Charnicia E. Huggins, "Mom's Worry Over Kid's Weight Ups Child's Fat Risk," Reuters Health (February 27, 2002) Source: American Journal of Clinical Nutrition 75 (March 2002): 451-452, 581-586. The writers sources can be found online at: http://www.ajcn.org/cgi/ (accessed March 20, 2008).

[10] TIME/ABC News Summit on Obesity, June 2-4, 2004, http://www.time.com/time/2004/obesity/ (accessed March 11, 2008).

matters worse. My own personal experience became a political issue.

The Project will be a large multimedia installation comprised of several smaller works of art. The centerpiece of the installation will consist of a seven-foot tall, approximately five-foot round papier-mâché statue of the Venus of Willendorf said to be the oldest naturalistic representation of a human being.[11] In 1908 the Austrian archaeologist Josef Szombathy found the Venus of Willendorf about 90 feet (30 meters) above the Danube River, near the town of Willendorf in Austria. Thought to have been made between 24,000 and 22,000 B.C.E., it has been called a Paleolithic Venus. Similar naked female figurines, usually less than 4" (10 cm) in height, and made of stone or ivory, have been found on many sites. While breasts, buttocks, and stomachs are voluminous, hands, feet, and faces are neglected or not represented at all. Although conventional archaeologists often associate them with fertility rites, they are fat, not pregnant.

Because of her antiquity and exaggerated female form, the Venus of Willendorf quickly became an icon of prehistoric art and replaced other examples of Paleolithic art in introductory art history textbooks. Because she was both female and nude, she fit perfectly into the patriarchal paradigm of the history of art and, because she was also the earliest known representation of the human body at the time, she became a prototype.

---

[11] The *Venus of Hohle Fels* also known as the *Venus of Schelklingen* discovered in September of 2008 near Schelklingen, Germany has been determined to predate the Venus of Willendorf. Dated to between 40,000 and 35,000 years old making it the earliest known undisputed example of a human being in prehistoric art.

In the 1960s her image was adopted by the feminist art movement as an icon of female power, for her presence was physical evidence that perhaps there had been a time when women were revered as gods, or a society that was matriarchal as opposed to patriarchal. Her large, voluptuous form also added credence to feminists' arguments against institutionalized beauty standards, such as those espoused by the Miss America Pageant. Her image can still be found in jewelry and emblazoned on T-shirts, chocolates and fridge magnets. She has been and continues to be used to promote size acceptance, fertility, and the earth mother. As I did research on the Venus of Willendorf, I found that the use of her image now includes a more sinister message; not only is her image not employed to empower women, but more and more it has become a vehicle for selling the ideas of an increasingly fat-phobic society. Christopher L. C. E. Witcombe, in his 2000 essay "Women in Prehistory: The Venus of Willendorf," has even suggested that the name Venus was used in mock irony as, "Venus, of course, was the Classical Goddess of sexual love and beauty," hinting that the "Woman" of Willendorf (as she has now come to be called) was the opposite of that.[12]

The third, and truest, catalyst for this incarnation of my project was a short-lived commercial for some diet system. The commercial was so objectionable that it probably didn't air for more than a week or two thus I didn't get a chance to see it more than once or twice. After trying for some time to find the culprit, it seems no one would fess up to it. I mean it was blasphemous. It was a TV spot, with a man's voice-over that droned on about the dangers of obesity while

---

[12] Christopher L. C. E. Witcombe, "Women in Prehistory: The Venus of Willen-dorf," Images of Women in Ancient Art (2000, revised 2003). Available online: http://witcombe.sbc.edu/willendorf/willendorfdiscovery.html (accessed Oct 21, 2007).

a picture of the Venus of Willendorf rotated on the screen. The voice asked viewers if they really wanted to look like her. Some ad man (it could only have been a man) had appropriated one of the most powerful symbols in women's history as a means of selling self-hatred and promoting patriarchal body-loathing ideals.

Regardless of how modern society views the Venus of Willendorf, she is by far the most realistic representation of my physical body that I have seen in the public domain, far more realistic than the images one sees in fashion magazines or in film and television. Nor is she headless, the way the media likes to depict fat people on the street and in society. [13] I intend to reclaim her as an honest depiction of what dieting and weight obsession does to the human body by making her the centerpiece of The Venus of Willendorf Project.

I am collecting discarded diet books to use as the sole source for the papier-mâché from which my Venus will be constructed. However, not all the books I have collected are suitable for the medium of papier-mâché. High-gloss paper, often used in the printing of cookbooks, for instance, does not take the glue very well,

---

[13] Charlotte Cooper, "Headless Fatties" image collection, "Images Collected by Charlotte Cooper." Available online: httpcharlottecooper.net/docs/fat/headless_fatties.htm (accessed March 11, 2008). If you've watched any news segment about fat people, ever, you've undoubtedly seen the video that accompanies such news segments: the parade of headless fatties, fat people in public, shown from the neck down, voiceless, stripped of their humanity—most likely without their permission. Showing people's bodies without their heads implies that it's shameful to be fat, that we ought to be ashamed to show our faces in public. COFRA, the Coalition for Fat Rights Activists, has started a video project called Dare to Show Your Face which invites people to upload a video of themselves that shows who they really are in their real lives—with their heads attached.

so books of this nature will be used to create a landscape or environment that will surround the central Venus figure. Smaller figures of the Venus will also be included in the installation. Each one represents a particular diet, and each Venus is made from copies of one particular book or author. For example, the Atkins Venus is entirely made of Atkins books. The Dr. Phil Venus and a Venus of Powter / Stop the Insanity Venus are completely constructed from the diet books of the two authors. The weight of each Venus will depend on how many of each author's books I have been able to collect.

In 2010 I displayed five such Venus Sculptures at the second annual ArtPrize in Grand Rapids Michigan. Filling a stage in a bookstore with my collection of over 8000 diet books while Venus of Fonda, Venus of Tarnower, Venus of Simmons, The Last Chance Venus and the Stop the Insanity Venus watched on as I actively worked on the central Venus, the Diet Deity. At seven feet tall and five feet around, in the end she will contain one copy each of every soft cover diet book I find. Her base and frame weigh what I weighted when I started this project, 375 pounds or 170 kilos. With each diet, like many of us do, she too has gained weight.

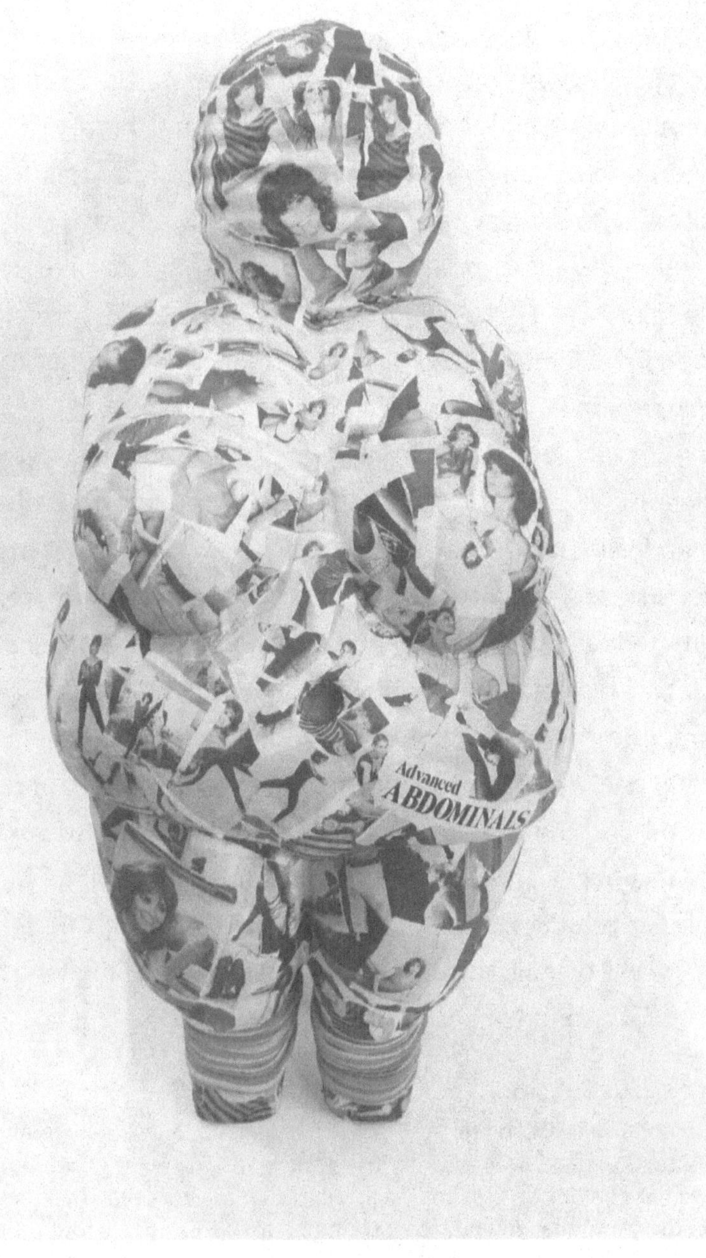

Advanced
ABDOMINALS

In February of 2013 I participated in an exhibition at Whitdel Arts in Detroit, MI called "Anywhere but Here." For my part, I installed the diet books in a life-size, one-passage, no-exit maze. The piece entitled "Diet Detour" was a multimedia installation that included elements to tease all the senses. Food smells, and an audio component were piped in. The sound consisted of droning thoughts about hunger and restriction. On display in February of that year, I figured that many people would have already broken their weight loss and fitness New Year's resolutions or be close to "falling off the wagon." What a brilliant time for viewers to find themselves trapped in a space filled with the overwhelming reality of the dieter's dilemma. "Do I go on feeling hungry or give in to temptation? What advice do I follow, there is so much misinformation it is like being a rat in a trap." This has led to a much clearer vision of The Venus of Willendorf Project's final manifestation. "Diet World" will be a life-size maze entirely constructed of diet books. Each passageway will represent a different eating disorder with walls that undulate depending on the dieter's weight. Thoughts will be pumped into each passage, giving the visitor an opportunity to wander through the mind as it is of someone with Anorexia or Binge Eating Disorder. Some passages might become too narrow for the average visitor to pass through. Others might end abruptly as someone with bulimia might die of cardiac complications due to binging and purging. The center of the maze will contain the different Venus sculptures in a kind of grotto[14] of self-acceptance.

---

[14] Canadian artist and fat activist Zoë Schneider in a recent installation "This Grotto Breathes" described her frustration with the word "grotesque" being used to describe fatness and fat art. In response she researched the root of the word "grotesque" to find that it stemmed from the word "grotto." Both words from the 1610s Italian grotto, Grotesque (adj.)" wildly formed, of irregular pro-portions, boldly odd" c. 1600s, originally a noun (1560s) (16c, Modern French

One benefit of working with papier-mâché is that it is lightweight. But with each subsequent layer it becomes stronger and heavier. This works as a physical metaphor for what happened to me with each subsequent diet: I gained more and more weight. With each diet book I add, the Venus too, will gain weight. Over the years some diets have been more popular than others, and there are more books promoting them, which have then ended up on the used book market. It is the smaller Venus sculptures made from one single author or title that I would like the viewer to be able to weigh—literally—to see which diet is the "best." Would it be the one that weighed the least? Or would it be the one that weighed the most, as so many were published and sold? Personally, I grew tired of weighing my success as a person on a bathroom scale. Perhaps we should be weighing the diet industry and all the

grotesque), from Italian grottesco, literally "of a cave" from grotto (see grotto) Online Etymology Dictionary. https://www.etymonline.com/word/grotesque (accessed December 13, 2020) misinformation it sends our way, and my installation will allow the viewer to do just that.

Before: I will encourage visitors to feel the difference in the weights of each of the individual sculptures, either simply by physically picking up the sculpture or by actually placing the piece on a scale.

After: I will encourage visitors to feel the difference in the weight of each individual sculpture, either by physically picking up the sculpture or by placing the piece on a scale.

The central Venus figure will be compiled of a multitude of different books, titles and authors including at least one copy of each book used to make the smaller pieces. There will be a separate inventory for this central piece, as well as an inventory for each of the smaller ones. I am compiling a complete inventory of all the books I incorporate into each statue and a bibliography that will catalog the books that are used in the project as a whole. I feel that this is the most historically responsible way to destroy the books physically without destroying the record of their existence. The evidence of all the books that were required to complete the creation of this installation allows the viewers truly to understand the enormity of the problem since "overweight" and "obesity" have become an issue to be resolved.

We are taught from childhood on to hate our bodies when there is nothing "wrong" with them. I can't even empty my bladder in the morning (while listening to the radio) without hearing at least three ads for some new diet product. "Eat all you want and still lose weight. We could not say it on TV if it wasn't true!!! Go to eatallyouwantandstillloseweight.com," Green Tea, Hoodia, it's never ending. The problem has gotten worse. I wonder, perhaps, if the so-called cure, and the multi-billion-dollar industry that has been created to resolve this "problem," is the cause. (Perhaps instead of suing fast-food chains we should start suing diet doctors and authors of diet books.) Diets make people fat.[15] The diet industry and all its money is actually feeding its own face. By making us feel dissatisfied with our bodies and obsess about our size, the diet industry is actually making the problem worse, capitalizing on our despair.

We have been hearing for a while now that diets don't work, even from the diet authors themselves,[16] so when are we going to stop buying their crap? Perhaps when people can visually experience the volume of the issue by standing at the center of this installation,

---

[15] Alison Field, ScD, Brigham and Women's Hospital researcher, says: "At a time when we need solutions to encourage healthy eating habits, it is troubling to see that dieting, which is often characterized by short-term and not necessarily healthy changes in eating, is so common…Our study found that dieting was counterproductive—children who dieted gained more, and not less, weight than non-dieters." "Dieting May Actually Promote Weight Gain in Children; Study Finds About 30 Percent of Girls and 16 Percent of Boys Diet, but Habit May Hold Little Hope for Long-term Success." Available online:
http://www.hms.harvard.edu/news/pressreleases/bwh/1003childdiet.html (accessed March 11, 2008).
University of Minnesota researchers analyzed the results of surveys conducted among teenagers from 1999 to 2004 to understand the perplexing finding that has been reported in several longitudinal studies, whereby dieting predicts greater weight gain over time in adolescents. Researchers led by Professor Dianne Neumark-Sztainer concluded that dieting might lead to weight gain in part because of the long-term adoption of behavioral patterns that are counterproductive to weight management, e.g., binge eating, decreased physical activity and a trend toward decreased breakfast consumption and decreased fruit and vegetable intake. "Dieting May Cause Weight Gain in Teenagers." Available online: http://www.earthtimes.org/articles/show/40693.html (accessed March 11, 2008).
[16] Bob Schwartz, *Diets Don't Work: Stop Dieting Become Naturally Thin Live a Diet-Free Life*, 3rd ed. (Houston, TX: Breakthru Publishing, 1996).

they will be able to feel the weight and the pressure in both a physical and intellectual way.

Imagine yourself in a room that is filled with diet books up the walls, cluttering the floors in mounds and mounds—where, in the center of the gallery, there is this giant iconic Venus larger than life. Interspersed amid the landscape of diet books there are the smaller Venus sculptures, leaning, resting, propped throughout the installation. My collection of diet books has not made a dent in the multi-billion-dollar industry that continues to publish and promote diet after diet. "How's that working for you?" to quote Phil McGraw, TV pop psychologist and star of the Dr. Phil Show. Dr. Phil McGraw likes to use this phrase when his guests continue to do things that are not working for them, and he and his son have both put out their own diet books, so in a sense he represents the diet industry. Is it working for us??? Hell NO!

Although papier-mâché is relatively cheap, the books from which I am acquiring the paper are not. That is why the Internet has proved to be the perfect place to get my materials. I can trade unwanted books for the diet books online.

Some of the books I have found are so priceless or unique that I have decided to treat them in rather a different manner. Some I have conserved in frames, maintaining their legibility with a humorous disclaimer that reads "In Emergency, Break Glass." Of all the elements of this installation, this best represents my personal relationship with dieting. Eating disorders don't just go away. They are with you forever, hanging there in the back of your mind, and can be triggered by the smallest of internal or external stimuli. An invitation to a party, an upcoming school reunion, a family function, meeting an old friend, a picture in a magazine, my own reflection in a shop window can all trigger obsessive thoughts of negative body image and food restriction, which in the past led to drastic and dangerous steps in an attempt to recapture a slender body from an earlier time.

For the most part, making diet books into papier-mâché seemed like the best treatment for the books. I wanted them destroyed and virtually unreadable except for the evidence that they had once been diet books. I will leave the sculpture unpainted so that people can read some of the type on the outer layers of the finished piece. There is a long history of papier-mâché being used in art, and as a medium it has extra-special significance for this piece. Papier-mâché is a French term that means "chewed paper." Not only does that metaphorically describe how I devoured these books in my earlier years, but it reminds me of a crazy diet tip I once read online, probably on some Pro-Ana (Pro-Anorexia) or Pro-Mia (Pro-Bulimia) Web site, about models chewing and swallowing facial tissue and cotton balls as a way to fill themselves up so they couldn't consume more food calories. I wonder how many calories there are in seven cotton balls? The fact that papier-mâché has been used in political art in Italy for centuries is also significant.

The Internet is an intoxicating place. I can be lost for hours searching for inspiration and imagery for my art there. For the Venus Project, however, I decided to use the computer not for ideas and images but as a means of acquiring my materials. It's not my only source; I still go to garage and yard sales and scour used bookstores and recycle centers, but the Internet has proved to be the best source. Not only have I been able to find large numbers of books for the project, but at the same time I am spreading the word about my project worldwide. People as far away as India have contributed to the piece. It has become a community project not unlike Judy Chicago's Dinner Party. (Contributions by many supporting artisans helped make Judy Chicago's famous installation, The Dinner Party, possible. Created during the years 1974-1979, The Dinner Party now has a permanent home at the Brooklyn Museum of Art.) By contributing books to the project people are taking part in the installation's creation. Not only is the Internet a great way to get advanced PR, but people are constantly giving me feedback. Good or bad, their responses inspire me to go on.

Over the years my work has more and more engaged in examples such as these described above. Commonly referred to as Social Practice. Annually for International No Diet Day I try to find ways to take my work out into the public forum. Engaging individuals in unsuspected ways. From stamping currency with non-diet messages, chalk graffiti and a plan for 2021 that will engage 50 fat activists across the United States in distributing free 10 artist made tabletop signs that read "Thank you for not talking about your diet," Venus of Willendorf Project. There will be 500 in total.

When I first decided to use diet books as my medium I went immediately to the Web, posting my call for unwanted diet books on different message boards:

Starving Artist Seeks Diet Books [emoticon]: Hi any and everyone...

I am an artist who is looking for any unwanted diet books to use in an installation piece I am working on... they can be in any condition hard cover or soft cover... repeats are great... the more the merrier... I will gladly pay for the shipping. I hope to hear from some of you soon.

My ad has not really changed much over the course of the project. I thought I was quite witty when early on I thought of the "Starving Artist Seeks Diet Books" caption, so that has always been my byline. As I have become more knowledgeable about fat politics, NAAFA National Association to Advance Fat Acceptance (NAAFA), Health at Every Size (HAES), and Fat Studies (something that came directly from this project, I might add), I started to use the phrase "Health at Every Size." It was on Web sites like these, NAAFA and the Fat Studies Listserv, that I posted my next call for books. Of course, most of these people had long purged themselves of diet books, but the community and support I have found there is priceless. I had the pleasure of sharing breakfast with Marilyn Wann, the author of FAT SO! She invited me to join her Listserv and post my call for books. It was from one of the women on this Listserv that I was introduced to an online community specifically for trading used books.

In 2015, for International No Diet Day, which has become increasingly important to putting my project out there, I did my most extravagant pitch for diet books yet by placing a full-page ad in the National Enquirer asking people to send me their diet books in honor of No Diet Day. Although it did not bring in as many books as I had hoped, (I got more love letters from prison then books) it attracted a fair amount of attention and to this day provides me with bragging rights that I once appeared naked in a national tabloid for two weeks.

When I think about how many diet books I have already amassed for the project, it is truly astounding. I have not even scratched the surface and my studio is already filled to the ceiling with books. I can't imagine what all the diet books in the world would look like. One often reads about the multi-billion-dollar diet industry, but what does that mean? To see it in paper, pages and pages of books, titles, the number of natural resources that are used in the publishing of this nonsense and self-hatred-provoking drivel, is unbelievable. To experience a room filled with it—to feel its weight and power—might really change how one thinks about dieting in the future and the personal waste. People will reconsider their choices when faced with the deluge of diet books that come out at the beginning of the New Year each year. They will start looking at themselves less harshly and come to accept that we all come in different colors, shapes and sizes and they will embrace their differences, (like many women artist have come to do in this fourth wave of feminism.)

This is a very personal project for me. Writing this essay and organizing my thoughts about this installation has taken me to an emotional depth that one finds mainly in the work of other women artists. I have no intention of neutralizing the subject; I want to be identified as revealing my femaleness and my fatness. For women artists that started the feminist art movement in the 1960s and 1970s, expressing one's female aesthetic, one's feminist sensibility was considered a trap, in that it would hold the artist back and lead to marginalization. Their determination and hard work have created an environment where it is no longer necessary to "paint like a man" to achieve recognition. In fact, many male artists have taken to using some intrinsically female modes of expression, for example sewing, baking and craft medium to employ in their own art works.

My hope is that my project will lead to the knowledge that diets don't work. They will see that we are being fed a load of bunk in regard to the "war on obesity," and that it is no longer necessary for women to maintain a slender figure, like sexless hangers for unwearable fashions in order to qualify as beautiful, worthwhile, valuable human beings. If I now have the freedom to make art like a woman, I should now have the freedom to have hips and a belly and breasts that sag like a woman. I am the Venus!

Belonging

Anique Radiant Heart

Yesterday, I experienced what I have waited for, for 42 years... I went to the place where the Venus of Willendorf was found... on top of a hill overlooking the small village of Willendorf.

When I was 28, I went to a workshop which changed my life forever. At that workshop, I saw a poster of the Venus of Willendorf. My heart almost stopped and I was filled with a sense of "belonging" that changed me at a visceral level.

When I saw that shape, I saw what I saw every time I stepped out of the shower – my big abundant body. I saw in that tiny figurine, all the healing and validation I needed to understand that my "bigness" must have been OK at some stage. That at some time... long long ago, it was revered to be large and bountiful and most importantly – a woman. And the fact that she was at least 40,000 years old, and represented the Goddess, in what was a global phenomenon at the time, made her doubly powerful to me. The Venus became a "touchstone" of all that is right and good about being a woman and being a Goddess woman.

Yesterday, accompanied by 4 gorgeous sisters, we journeyed to Willendorf and offered our love to the Venus and to the land and to the Ancestors who worshiped Her. On top of a beautiful hill, with the Twin Peaks – the breasts of the Goddess before us and the River Danube flowing below us, we created ceremony and offered our blessings, our gratitude to the Goddess as Venus and to the Place and Divas of the Land.

At the top of the hill, each sister offered prayers and blessings. As we left, each of us sat on the Omphalos Stone—which had been carefully preserved and placed perfectly so that (when we sat upon it)—it appeared to line up with the base of the yoni, while the mountains in the background framed the picture.

Then we progressed below to the riverbank, where beautiful Eva Cornelia placed a chair she had brought for me so I could enjoy the breathtaking scenery and the feel of the river at my feet.

After some swimming, the sisters created a stone cairn – altar – and we each found a stone into which we imbued something we wished to release for this week, and then throw in the river to be "dissolved" and carried away. As always, these rituals are so profound—as each sister speaks her truth in trust, and is witnessed by others. I was moved very deeply.

The magic of the synchronicity of meeting the Venus at her place of recognition, at a time when I am finally meeting and getting to know and love my body, is not lost on me.

The Old Rounded Crone

Trista Hendren

On a hill far away, stood an old rounded Crone,
The emblem of all we revered.
And I love that old Crone who resembles me now,
After decades of love and babies.

So I'll cherish the old rounded Crone,
Till my shame, I at last, lay down.
I will cling to the old rounded Crone,
Till I learn how to love all I am.

See they taught us to hate, any fat on ourselves,
Our mothers and grandmother's shamed.
For they wanted us small, and to deal with it all,
While they stole our divinity.

So I'll cherish the old rounded Crone,
Till my shame, I at last, lay down.
I will cling to the old rounded Crone,
Till I learn how to love all I am.

Oh, that old rounded Crone so despised by the world,
Has a wondrous attraction for me.
For the dear Willendorf, left Her body to love,
To show us how grand we can be.

So I'll cherish the old rounded Crone,
Till my shame, I at last, lay down.
I will cling to the old rounded Crone,
Till I learn how to love all that I am.

In the old rounded Crone, stain'd with blood so divine,
A wondrous beauty I see.
For she laid it all bare, without need for despair,
So boldly proclaiming I AM!!

So I'll cherish the old rounded Crone,
Till my shame, I at last, lay down.
I will cling to the old rounded Crone,
Till I learn how to love all that I am.

Now the old rounded Crone, bears my Nana's lost hopes,*
She tells me there are other ways.
You see long, long ago, before men had a go,
Women were H-O-L-Y.

So I'll cherish the old rounded Crone,
Till my shame, I at last, lay down.
I will cling to the old rounded Crone,
Till I learn how to love all that I am.

There is never a day, I don't miss my Nano,*
But in Willendorf, she I still see.
Then She'll call me some day to our Goddess estate,
Where Her hugs I'll forever embrace.

So I'll cherish the old rounded Crone,
Till my shame, I at last, lay down.
I will cling to the old rounded Crone,
Till I learn how to love all that I am.

Trista's re-write of The Old Rugged Cross, written by George Bennard in 1912 was inspired by Anique Radiant Heart's photographic description of her beautiful journey in Austria.

*Nana was my maternal grandmother, JoAnne, and Nano was my paternal grandmother, Marge. While I still miss them both every day, they still come to me often in my dreams—in all their Willendorf-ish glory.

Willendorf Banner

Lydia Ruyle

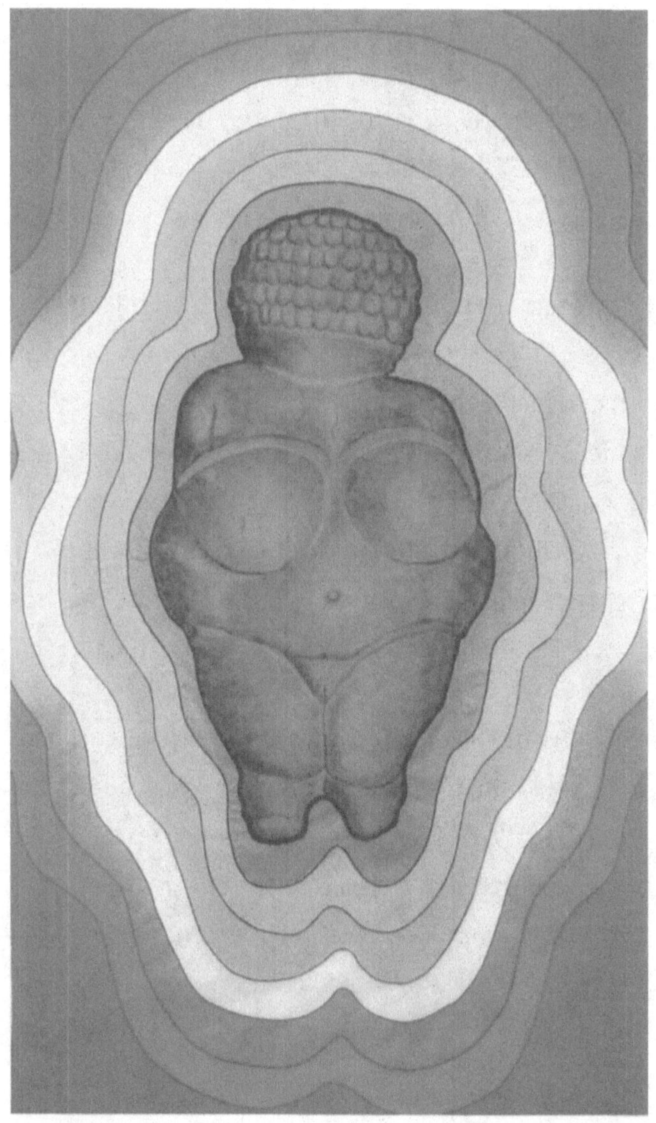

Photo courtesy of the film *Herstory: The Visionary Life of Lydia Ruyle and the Banners of the Divine Feminine* by Isadora Leidenfrost, PhD. A Soulful Media Production. 2019.

They are not "Venus" Figurines[17]

Max Dashu

I've spent fifty years studying the cultural record, searching for societies where women were free, and attempting to decolonize the history (and myths about history) that have been handed down as "truth" in the narratives of "Western Civilization" (and other patriarchies).

Scanning through archaeological reports, I found that the farther back in time I looked, the more female figurines appeared in the excavations. In fact, these ancient statuettes—in stone, ivory, bone, and ceramic—turned out to be the central icons of the paleolithic and neolithic. They are the earliest human representations—and they are overwhelmingly female. In 2008, I created the poster "Female Icons, Ancestral Mothers" to demonstrate the global scope of these ancient female icons, from the paleolithic to recent times.

It took decades of digging through obscure specialist journals to find out how global this phenomenon was. Caught up in their search for rulers, chieftains, and weapons, writers and editors disregarded this female iconography. They often deemed the cultures where the female icons were prominent as unimportant and unworthy of notice. Writers commonly dismissed the small female icons as toys, "dancing girls," or "concubines" and, most

---

[17] "They are not "Venus" figurines" was originally published on Facebook. You can share it there by searching for the title on the Suppressed Histories Archives Facebook page. ©2020 Max Dashu

commonly of all, as "fertility idols." Even now, archaeologists and other academics persist in reducing them to this stereotype, using "fertility idol" as their term of choice. But that phrase flattens out a richer examination of their cultural and spiritual significance. It is tainted with the anti- "idolatry" prejudices of patriarchal religions, but with a veneer of scientific "objectivity."

The widely used term "Venus figurine" also imposes an alien interpretative framework, and not only because of its eurocentrism. It projects a narrow modern presumption of "sex object" onto iconography that has a far broader range of meanings and ceremonial uses. Some will say, "But Venus was a Goddess—what's wrong with that?" Few people are even aware that this naming originates from the Marquis de Vibraye's sardonic description of a small paleolithic statuette found in 1864 on his Laugerie-Basse estate in Dordogne. The classically-educated aristocrat called her a "Vénus impudique," seeing her as "immodest" in contrast to the Roman archetype of Venus Pudica.

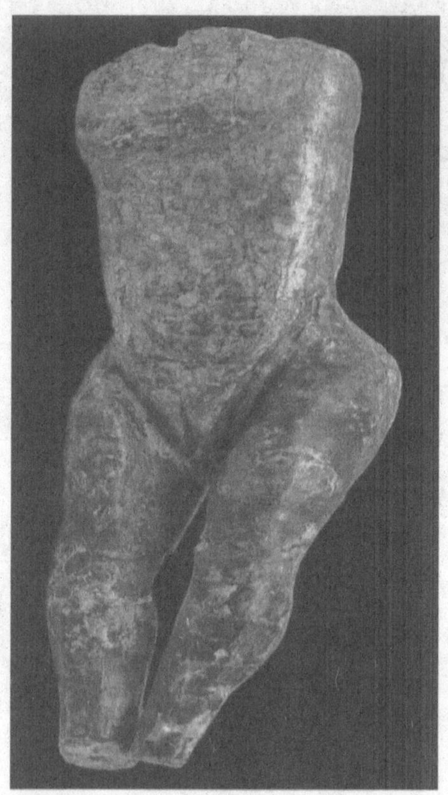

The mammoth ivory icon of Laugerie-Basse, 8 cm.

You'll have seen some of the many statues of Venus covering her genitals with one hand and her breasts with the other in a gesture of shame. In fact, *pudica* translates to "shame" as well as "modesty," and the etymology ultimately goes back to "shrinking," as Venus visibly does in the statues. The word *pudendum* comes from the same Latin root *pudenda* ("that whereof one ought to feel shame"), which historically was used far more commonly of the vulva than of male genitalia. These icons of a far more ancient era represent the opposite of this mentality of a patriarchal male gaze. They are self-contained and potent, having grown out of an entirely different cultural reality.

Two Roman sculptures of Venus Pudica, who embodies shame and fear.

The modern classifications foreclose consideration of the real significance of the female icons. They fail to address the probability that they represented female ancestors, as comparison with more recent examples would suggest. They fail to consider the ceremonial context of the figurines, or their connective and collective valence, in contrast to the social hierarchies that so many anthropologists were looking for.

By far the most famous of these ancient icons is
She of Willendorf.

The patriarchal assumptions in "processual" analysis have cast a long shadow over interpretation of the ancient icons. They never attempt to address the existence of Indigenous matricultures, much less the importance of matrilineal ancestors in those societies, in ceremony as well as iconography. Instead, the prevailing nomenclature imposes a lens that is both patriarchalizing and eurocentric. They present us not only with "the Venus of Willendorf," but also the "Venus of Curayacú" (Peru), "Venus of Kondon" (Manchuria), "Jomon Venus" (Japan), and countless others. (While repudiating this modern-day *interpretatio romana,* I would like to credit the Italian scholars who, like many Eastern Europeans, have been far more willing to acknowledge the sacrality of the ancient female icons than their counterparts in Anglophone academia, for example in the US, UK, Australia.)

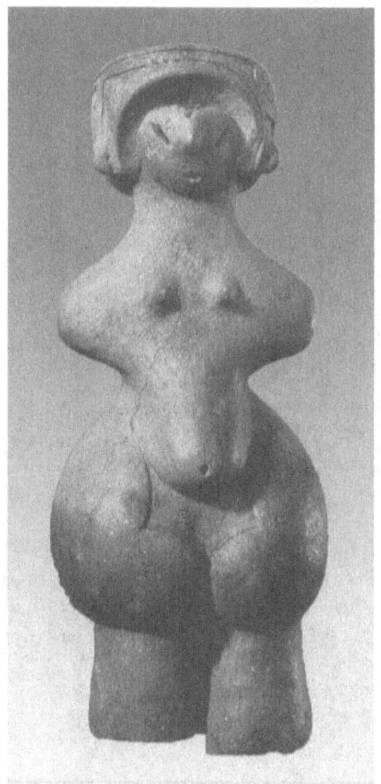

A net search shows this figure is often
described as "the Jomon Venus."

But while it's necessary to analyze the assumptions embedded in the discourse about the ancient icons, that is secondary to making the full archaeological picture known and visible to the public. Our task is to restore women to cultural memory, to learn and reveal what has been hidden from view. It is not about high theory or abstruse terminology. This study of the disregarded female icons leads us into revelatory litanies of place-names and cultural horizons: Badarian, Naqada, Halafian, Chasseyan, Jomon, Yarmukian, Saladoid, Barrancoid; Harappa, Mohenjo-Daro, Kulli and Merhgarh; Niuheliang, al-Ubaid, Samarra and Hassuna, Be'ersheva; Chalcatzingo, Las Bocas, Tlatilco, Chupícuaro; Nicoya-Guanacaste; Valdivia, Marajó and Tapajós, Condorhuasi; Anau, Kultepe, and all the other Tepe-mounds of Iran and Turkmenistan, and the tells of Iraq and the Levant.

From Harappa, Pakistan,
early 3rd millennium bce.

Going further back in time, we find Hohle-Fels, Dolni-Vestonice, Laussel, Brassempuy, Balzi Rossi, Chiozza, Savignano. Yes, of course, there is Willendorf, and also Kostienki, Gagarino, and Mal'ta, in Siberia. Even earlier come the stone figures of Tan-tan in Morocco, and Berekhet Ram in Israel/Palestine. The well-known artifacts of Çatal Höyuk and Hacilar are supplemented by lesser-known but extremely rich Anatolian sites like Kösk Höyuk and Bademagaci. We scan the better-known horizons of Old Europe— Karanovo, Sesklo, Cucuteni-Tripillye, Vinca—as well as bronze age Mesopotamia, and the far less-publicized record of Sudan, from the deep neolithic into the early centuries CE.

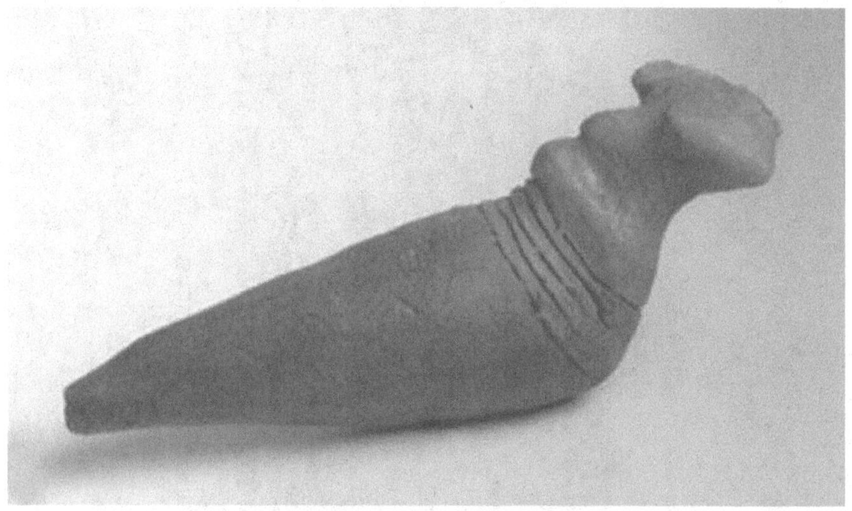
Sudan, circa 3000 bce, from the socalled "A-Group."

Many of these heritages come to us labeled with colonial exonyms: the "A-Group" of neolithic Sudan, the "Basketmaker" culture of the ancient Pueblos, or the so-called "Fremont culture" of Utah. (We really need a better name for that one than a military officer who played a key role in colonizing lands west of the Rockies.) From Illinois to Ohio, the figurines and sites of the Mississippian cultures all got named after European settlers who took these lands: "Hopewell," "Turner Mound," the "Mann site." There must be a more culturally evocative title for the tiny figurines of "Poverty Point," Louisiana, or the large ones of the Inland Delta of the Niger in Mali. It is difficult to identify site names for those, or for their predecessors in the Nok culture of Nigeria, or the millennia-old figurines in Zimbabwe. But the important thing is knowing that they exist, and being able to see their form.

From southern Ohio, the "Turner Mounds," circa 500 CE.

One of my students asked me recently, "So what should we call them then?" My short answer was "female icons," which conveys their sacred valence while preserving the broadest possible spectrum of meanings. That has been the simplest, clearest, and least-loaded naming that I have been able to come up with. But a multiplicity of possible names is needed, which is why I also use "ancestral mothers" or "ancestral women" or "paleolithic grandmothers." I sometimes still say "ancient figurines" or "female figurines," for maximum clarity about what artifacts I am referring too. It will take us a while to build a common language with referents understandable to everyone.

Anatolian icon from Hacilar, Turkey, more than 7,000 years ago.

In Japan the icons are called dogu, which some translate as "dolls," but literally means "clay figures." Because the English word "doll" has been used dismissively for so long in archaeological texts, it used to raise my hackles. But the Japanese archeaologists recognize their sacral import, and have documented their placement in shrine areas of houses. After thinking about this over decades, I realized that "sacred dolls" is a descriptive name that comes up in living Indigenous contexts: whether it is the female ancestor carvings called Mwana Hiti in Tanzania, or the Odas grandmother carvings of the Lenape in North America, where women keep the doll-making tradition alive. Such icons in wood or clay wrapped with grasses and beads represent female ancestors in womanhood initiations in some parts of South Africa. They figure in prayers and ceremonies for conception among the Ashanti and various other African peoples.[18] Ceremonial use of the small icons is indicated in a great many of the ancient archaeological contexts as well. The figurines themselves often give us a window into ritual paint-up, symbols, and regalia.

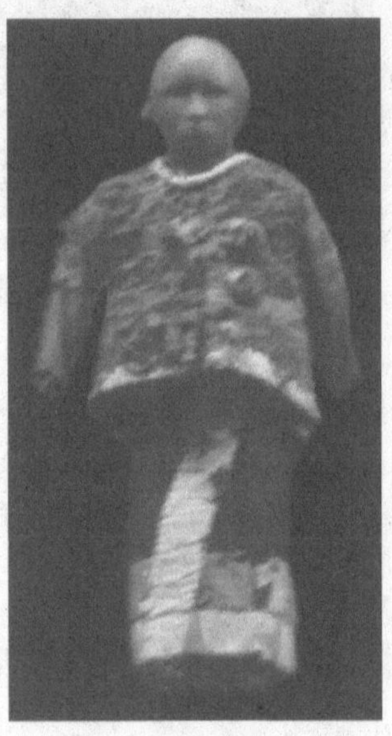

Odas Grandmother doll of the Lenape people,
American Indian Museum.

II.

Naming is so fraught and loaded with cultural implications and assumptions. I've been fighting the assumptions encoded in "fertility idols" and "Venus figures" for decades. In the 70s and 80s feminists and pagans called them "goddesses" because we recognized their sacrality and potency. We fought against the enforcers who claimed that the figurines were historically or

---

[18] See examples at https://en.wikipedia.org/wiki/African_dolls

culturally unimportant, and who treated anything Goddess as a kind of heresy not to be tolerated in academic discourse.

Our definition of Goddess is markedly different from theirs. We embraced her as immanent, unlike the distant and disembodied transcendent god of patriarchal religions, and we saw her as a spectrum: of Being, of beings, of consciousness in everything and through the cycles of life and death. We recognized her as verb, as transformative and transforming, and not a reified thing that stood separate and apart. And we recognized her as Ancestor, as untrammeled female potency.

Cucuteni-Tripillye culture,
Romania, Moldova, Ukraine

But this became complicated for reasons other than what the academic old guard was saying. Many Indigenous women objected to the Goddess nomenclature. Some prefer to speak of spirits, who could be primordial beings or nature spirits or ancestors. The Navajo refer to "the holy people," rather than to "gods and Goddesses." Often these beings are named in kinship terms, like Our Mother, or Old Woman Who Never Dies, among the Mandan. The Shawnee revered Our Grandmother, Kokomthena, who is Creator and clearly a deity.

There are a range of cultural approaches among the many ethnicities. In the Pueblo traditions, Spider Grandmother acts as a creator (see the writings of Leslie Marmon Silko and Paula Gunn Allen). Barbara Mann has laid out stories of co-creation by multiple beings (and this is not only true of the Iroquoian traditions). She views the coalescence by the 20th century of "Creator" discourse as the product of christianizing influence. I've read and heard North American traditions that speak of Creator in masculine terms, but in recent decades have noticed a shift, as prayers that used to be directed to Grandfather changing to Grandfather, Grandmother, or reversed. Which is how I've seen it in Mapuche prayers to the Grandmothers and Grandfathers of the East, South, West, and North.

This takes us down so many byways of language, which is a core constituent of culture and its philosophical underpinnings. Deity, divinity, *diosa, déesse, dea, dia, diva, devonna, devī, diwiya* all come from a Proto-Indo-European root that means "to shine." *Goddess* tacks on a Romance feminizing ending to a Germanic root which was not originally gendered as "god" came to be:

The Proto-Germanic meaning of *guđán and its etymology is uncertain. It is generally agreed that it derives from a Proto-Indo-European neuter passive perfect participle *ǵʰu-tó-m. This is similar to Persian word for God, Khudan. This form within (late) Proto-Indo-European itself was possibly ambiguous, and thought to derive from a root *ǵʰeu̯- "to pour, libate" (the idea survives in the Dutch word, 'Giet', meaning, to pour) (Sanskrit huta, see hotṛ), or from a root *ǵʰau̯- (*ǵʰeu̯h2-) "to call, to invoke" (Sanskrit hūta).[19]

What I find significant about *guđán* is that it spans address to divinities and to ancestors. So, when we trace back to root meanings for European names for Goddess, we find animacy (this reframing by Potawatomi botanist Robin Wall Kimmerer is most useful, because the colonialist prejudices attached to "animism" are problematic). There is "shining" (*deiwa/*deiwos) or there is "those to whom are made offerings, who are invoked, called in" (*guđán*) . Both these sets of meaning can apply to a spectrum of beings, from divinities to ancestors to land spirits who are embodied. And many instances exist in European cultures of addressing the Divine with kinship terms, from the Matronae and Matres stones of the Germans, Britons and Gauls, to the Welsh Y Mamau, a faerie naming that means "the mothers." Or we can think of the four dozen kinds of *māte* ("mothers") revered in Latvia, from Zēmys Māte (Mother Earth) to the numerous *māte* of sea, forest, sand, fire.

---

[19] https://en.wikipedia.org/wiki/God_(word)

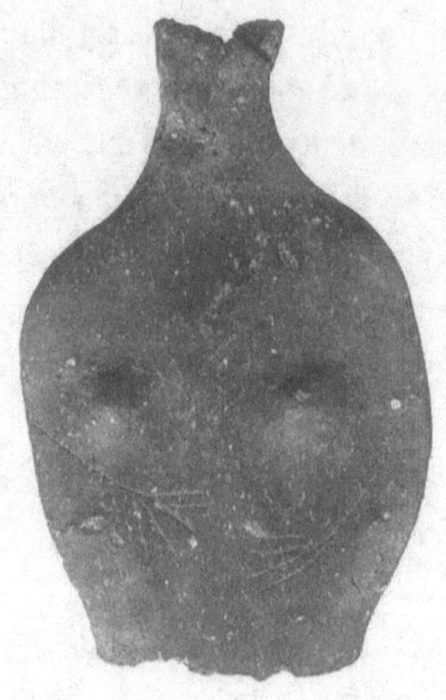

Chasseyan culture, Paris basin, circa 4000 bce

III. A historical lens on Venus

But I want to go back to the term "Venus," and the ways it has been used in modern times. Very little is known about archaic Venus among the Latins. No images of her survive other than the sexual / modesty polarity that the Romans (and Etruscans too) had absorbed from the Hellenes. The ethnic distinctions here were greater than is usually recognized. (How many people think of Saturnus as a god of agriculture, for example? He was for the Romans—very different than Greek Kronos. And who has ever heard of his wife Ops, once an important Latin Goddess, whose name means "plenty"?) Behind Venus herself is Aphrodite, and behind her stands the Semitic Goddess 'Ashtart / Astarte / Ishtar, all of them associated with the planet, as was Sumerian Inanna. In each cultural shift she changes—in an increasingly patriarchalizing direction.

The point here is how Venus was made into a stereotype for the male gaze, and understanding how that is not the same thing as actual female sexuality—no matter how many times they insist that it must be, and that patriarchal projections are (the only) reality. The highly sexualized Venus stereotype didn't stop with the Romans but was carried along in European art, through medieval and Renaissance and baroque and Romantic paintings and sculptures, as a normative way of looking at women's bodies, that even defined what women were. Male artists enthusiastically kept Venus Pudica going, holding her hands ineffectively over breasts and genitals, or limply reclining *en déshabille*, her head dropped, usually gazing down, or looking away somewhere in the distance. Only rarely does she look directly at you, as so many of the archaic figurines do, with their bold stance—their wide or fat bodies taking up space without shrinking or apology.

One thing that's striking about most of these images, whether it's Botticelli or Rubens or Goya, is how the knees of Venus are drawn tightly together, especially when she is standing. It's the same pose that fashion has trained women to assume. Just look at these, the defensive stance, the closed legs, and behind that, the fear of rape, the idea that a relaxed female body is somehow scandalous. Many women remember being scolded into keeping our knees together, our skirts drawn down, in stark contrast to socialized manspreading.

These negative encodings are cultural spells whose roots most women are totally unaware of, and yet they are deeply embedded in how we are taught to look and move and inhabit our bodies. And if we do not, there are consequences. If we do, there are other consequences. But these scripts die very hard. They're still being propagated. They are the cultural wallpaper of the dominant society. This is supposed to be "the sexy pose," and yet it is culturally specific, far from universal, and prescriptive in ways most have yet to recognize.

All those assumptions and projections are invoked when people refer to "Venus figurines," even if they aren't consciously aware of them.

IV. Racist beastialization

There's another aspect to this Venus terminology—an intensely racialized one. It was used as a racist insult and sexual mockery to describe a Khoekhoe woman, Sara Baartman, as "the Hottentot Venus." Her captors paraded her around freak shows in England, Ireland and France. (And she was not the only Khoekhoe woman treated in this manner, only the most famous one.) She died from this very lonely and alienating captivity among hostile strangers. This contemptuous and contemptible use of "Venus" was used to degrade Sara Baartman, and not her alone, but all the other African women subjected to this abuse.

Europeans published many horribly offensive cartoons of South African women from the late 1700s/early 1800s, contrasting them with white standards of beauty and femininity. They projected African women as "savages"—lacking in any rights, boundaries, or respect. This is what made it possible to traffic a Khoekhoe woman as an exotic "curiosity," cutting her off from her people and country, subjecting her to abuse and mockery and misery. "Sara was literally treated like an animal. There is some evidence to suggest that at one point a collar was placed around her neck." In 1814, she was sold to a French animal trainer:

> "Georges Cuvier, founder and professor of comparative anatomy at the Museum of Natural History, examined Baartman as he searched for proof of a so-called missing link between animals and human beings. [!] After being sold to S. Reaux she was raped, and impregnated by him as an experiment. The child was named Okurra Reaux, and she died at five years of age of an unknown disease.

> "After her death, [Georges] Cuvier dissected her body, and displayed her remains. For more than a century and a half, visitors to the Museum of Man in Paris could view her brain, skeleton and genitalia as well as a plaster cast of her body... Cuvier interpreted her remains, in accordance with his theories on racial evolution, as evidencing ape-like traits. He thought her small ears were similar to those of an orangutan and also compared her vivacity, when alive, to the quickness of a monkey.

> "Baartman lived in poverty, and died in Paris of an undetermined inflammatory disease in December 1815. Her remains were returned to South Africa in 2002 and she was buried in the Eastern Cape on South Africa's National Women's Day."[20]

---

[20] https://en.wikipedia.org/wiki/Sarah_Baartman

Intensely racist projections comparing Africans to apes were still alive in the 1930s, under the aegis of "Science." the South African government confined the !Xhosa prophetess Nomtetha Nkwekwe to a madhouse, for years, in order to suppress her leadership of a liberatory African movement. In researching her story, I read that doctors at that mental "hospital" were experimenting on African women, by attempting to transplant the uteri of baboons into their bodies. And this should remind us of the atrocities that Dr. Marion Simms committed against enslaved African women in the U.S. in the 1800s. He performed experimental "surgeries" on their uteri, without anesthesia, and certainly without consent. This man was hailed as the father of gynecology for his torture and exploitation of the unfortunate women who were placed into his hands.

The history of using "Venus" to ridicule, exploit and torment African women is yet another argument against perpetuating use of the term "Venus figurines." It is too heavily loaded with a history of degradation and misogynist objectification. For this and all the reasons I have given above, it is not an appropriate way of naming one of the most significant global patterns of female iconography. That rich cultural heritage needs to be recognized in all its diversity, and integrated into our understanding of history and spiritual culture.

Max Dashu, Suppressed Histories Archives

The poster Female Icons, Ancestral Mothers shows the global expanse of the ancient female figurines.
http://www.suppressedhistories.net/femaleicons.html

Female Icons, Ancestral Mothers – Max Dashu

Willendorfia

Sharon Smith

Wouldn't it be wonderful
to live in a land where chubby little Goddesses
with big boobs and big thighs
are considered beautiful?

Where women no longer feel ashamed
if their thighs rub together
when they walk,
or their boobs can't fully be restrained
by Barbie Doll bras?

What a land that would be!
What a marvel to live there
and love there
and celebrate our succulent ripeness
as full-bodied women.

Rather than force our voluptuousness
into shape-shifting Body Armor
To flatten us, mold us
and make us "acceptable"
(not to mention uncomfortable as hell).

I'd name it "Willendorfia," and all women,
large and small and everywhere
in between would be welcome.

I'd name it for my precious
Goddess of Willendorf,
that Chunky Monkey Goddess who
flaunts unapologetically her glorious
expansive body—Her belly, round
as the Earth itself;
Her breasts large enough
To feed a planet of hungry children.
Her vagina, round, moist,
and fertile: the holy portal through which
all souls passed into Life in all its
messy glory.

Willendorfia! Sweet Willendorfia,
Land of Naked, Dancing Women,
boobs flapping in the night air
as we dance together, bare-bellied,
bare-assed, around a blazing fire.

No shame here! No blame here!
No reason to feel uncomfortable
being naked here:
Your bodies are all the bodies of
The Great She.

And all of them are sexy, powerful,
beautiful and Goddessy!

All of them are magical, marvelous and
creative, so own them, Sisters:
every curve, every wrinkle, bulge and roll!

In Willendorfia, you are all Queens,
all revered... all FUCKING amazing!
In Willendorfia, you can wear that flowing mumu
or those tight spandex pants: Fit those clothes
to your glorious curves however you want!

Wouldn't it be wonderful
to live in a land where chubby little Goddesses
with big boobs and big thighs
are considered beautiful?

Wouldn't it be wonderful indeed!
And why shouldn't it be our reality?
What makes us think it's a pipe dream,
something unattainable, an elusive butterfly
just out of our reach?

I say, Look to the Goddess of Willendorf:
She will surely show us the way.

The Great Mother of All

Daniel Cox

Years ago, I started writing a story, a story of our creation. The image of the Venus of Willendorf has always entranced me— ever since I was a child really.

My spiritual path started early on at Sunday School. When I questioned why God was a man—and when I told the reverend I could hear Jesus (and the Devil) talking to me—I didn't last long.

For me, everything is alive. Being an animist means we develop a relationship with the spirits of the land, the rivers, the trees, the otherworld beings—even cars. But, the Goddess, the Divine Feminine, the Earth Herself, has always had my heart.

I remember several years ago, I was in the Goddess temple in Glastonbury. I remember feeling awkward sitting there in front of the many faces of She, including other women. I felt I didn't belong there. Then, all of a sudden, quite unexpectedly, tears started falling down my cheeks. Before I knew it, I was uncontrollably sobbing. I was gazing at an image of the Venus of Willendorf and I felt such a pull to open my heart to Her.

I dedicated my life to the Goddess at that moment—to help bring Her back into spirituality, into people's lives. The Venus of Willendorf was, is my vision.

I bought a large replica of Her when I was a student—it was an ex-museum piece. I spent a lot of my student loan on it—but I'm glad I did, despite the ever-growing debt the loan provides.

I knew what I had to do: I had to write; I had to paint. I had to offer my services to healing—including the healing of the wounded feminine within women and men, including myself.

I tried desperately to paint the image of Her, incorporating all that She is to me—but I couldn't. It was almost impossible. I gave up trying and instead, I just called Her in. I called in Her story and the image flowed.

So here it is. It wasn't something I ever planned on sharing, but when I did share it, something strange happened; some women began to cry. I realised that there may be something special about my art. In fact, it kick-started my path of being a visionary artist.

The image depicts the Mother Goddess, `Venus of Willendorf' giving birth to all things. Out of the sacred flood waters sprung the sun and the moon, the animals, then the first human people. The embryonic waters became the oceans and rivers and Her blood dried and became the rich soil. Her milk became the nourishment in the land and some droplets spilled and became the Milky Way. Above, the Watchers witnessed it all.

I am currently writing the book now. It has taken me a decade to get back to it, but it has adapted slightly. Here is an excerpt:

'Lonely, the Great Woman wandered the universe, her stomach was swollen, her breasts were heavy. Wearily she heaved her colossal weight around. In the dark she doubled up in pain as the first of many contractions waved through her. Fearfully she cried out in pain, her sore, dry lips cracked when she moaned. Again, and again they came and went, each time more painful, each time more intimidating, each time more agonising.

At last, her body was ready; she raised her holy thighs, twin pillars marking the entrance to the vast and sacred womb, with an almighty gush, the sacred floodwaters were sent forth. She gave birth to her first born, Somi the sun.

A serpent of golden light, so beautiful was his light, he lit up the universe. For the first time the Great Mother could see.

Our Mother's heart opened like a flower. She breathed a breath of life into his tiny body and like a nugget of coal he shone. She took him in her arms and fed him with her ample breasts. Tiny droplets of the nourishing milk spilled from his mouth, catching alight, they fell into the universe creating the stars we see, ancient fires of our ancestors.

While the bright babe was sleeping, she spun him around her body, like a tight little coil of fire and flame spinning about her. She was so overjoyed with her baby, so full of love for her first born, the pride of our Mother.

She enjoyed her time with her new love, caressing his tiny toes, stroking his soft skin and scales and kissing his little nose. His little face wrinkled up as he yawned a big sigh, but something felt different. Her body felt different; her breast became painful and there was a strange feeling between her legs. There was a feeling of warmth and a discomfort deep within. She looked down and saw blood pouring from her vulva.

In time this dried blood became the soil of our land. Her sacred water became the seas and lakes, her tears became the rivers and streams, her hair a tangle of plants and fields. Her recumbent body became the landscape and her womb became every opening into the sacred earth.

She became 'The Great Mother of All.'

I Remember My Heritage

Kat Shaw

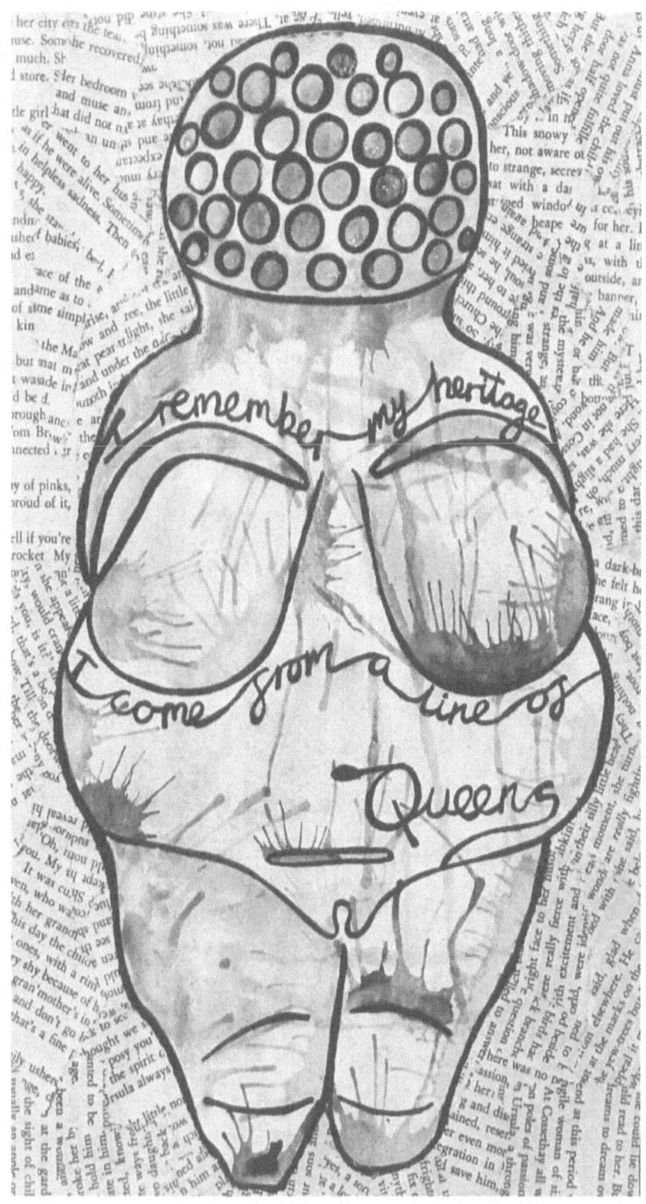

I Have My Mother's Face

Sharon Smith

I have my Mother's face…
There it is, in the mirror, staring back at me.
The same lines by the corners of my mouth…
The same receding, fading brown eyes…
The same "neck-waddle."
The same wrinkles.
The same grey hairs.

I have my Mother's face.

Once I vowed I would never look like her:
A regimen of face creams, hair dyes,
buffers, scrubbers—Exfoliate it away!
Poisoning my body to deny my DNA.
Fighting against Time to be "young"
when what did Youth ever do for me?

What did I learn during those years?
But to be a Puppet of the Patriarchy;
bearing a burden of perfection
upon my shoulders
too heavy for me to carry and
too hard for me to support.

What did I get from it?
Not the Wisdom I now have.
Not the Grace or Compassionate Understanding.

Not the Wild Woman fire that burns in my soul,
born of years of Struggle and Pain
to discover Who I Am.

I have my Mother's face.
Her eyes look back at me, and I weep.
Not tears of sorrow for the face I now see,
but tears of remorse that I once despised
this beautiful face; once thought it ugly,
a thing to be ashamed of, because
I had bought into the Patriarchal Lie.

I have my Mother's face.
Societal "Norms of Beauty" be damned!
Restricted, conflicted Womanity
noosed about the neck and dragged along
for how many centuries,
sculpting, molding our bodies to be
"Acceptable" and "Worthy of Love."
This face I ran from...
This face is ME!

I have my Mother's face.
The face of the Crone,
The Grandmother,
The Elder Woman,
The Wise Woman,
The Matriarch.
The Wild Woman,
The Goddess!

I have my Mother's face.

It is mine.

I have inherited it.

I have earned it.

And, by the Goddess,

I shall wear it proudly!

And I shall honor it for all of

the days left to me.

I have my Mother's face.

She was a Goddess, you see…
And so am I.

Birth of the Conscious Feminine

Dr. Leonor Murciano-Luna

Every time we think of dieting to make our bodies smaller, or we commit to a surgical cosmetic procedure to alter our body—chasing some imaginary ideal of what would be better, we abandon ourselves and our bodies. This is where we're controlled by the patriarchal norms and conditioning.

We may think that these thoughts are innocent and that we're just subscribing to what we want. The truth is that behind what we want is a perceptual reality at play, which is being informed and manipulated by the constant media manipulation of what we should be, along with the misleading pattern of 'we would be better off if', 'we would be more fulfilled if', etc. And most of us unconsciously buy into this message, believing that we have autonomy in making these decisions. These are the underlying messages that we are buying into when we follow through on the behaviors that are supported by those thoughts. Nevertheless, we shouldn't be too quick to judge ourselves, because these are deeply ingrained patterns of survival behavior, that mostly continue to influence us, unconsciously. And so, the work is to awaken to these patterns of manipulation within ourselves, to unplug from them, and free ourselves from the control of this spell.

For example, let's take a look at the collective view of the issue of women's weight. This has been an interesting and very personal arena for myself—as it has with most women. For most of us who gain weight during various life changes—giving birth, menopause, etc.—there's a subtle judgment that appears where we are encouraged to lose weight and return to the weight that our bodies were at one time. There's very little regard for the process the body has undergone, rather it seems that it's usually reduced to this single idea of 'having to lose weight and return to the past', as if accomplishing this, the body would somehow be better off. What about the wisdom, the sacredness, and the transformation that the body has undertaken during this time? These things aren't valued in our society, therefore, they are usually not mentioned, even in our own minds.

Submitting to this thinking of returning to the body's past weight, or even deciding that the body has a particular weight it should be, is in itself a denial of the state of the body in the present moment. Not only that but it is clearly buying into an arbitrary idea of what the body should look like at any given moment, making it wrong if it doesn't meet up to those standards.

This is a complete denial and rejection of the body's state, and a complete conformity to the patriarchal ideal of a woman's body. Unknowingly, we continuously give the message to our body that it was wrong in the shape and size that it is showing up. And then proceed with layering feelings of failure, powerlessness and inadequacy because we don't meet the standards of some illusionary objectified ideal.

At the end of the day, we have severed the trust with our bodies— and this is the relationship we are rebuilding as we unplug ourselves from the umbilical dependency and expectations we have been immersed in. Is it possible to trust my body's innate wisdom, more than the conditioned norms that have been imposed on me throughout my lifetime? This is the question we are faced with every time; we consider unplugging and not following through on one of these impulses. Will we let fear stop us? We will let shame make us feel desperate enough for us to give in? This is the personal conflict we embark on when we dare to disengage from the cultural conditioned patterns.

Excerpt from *Birth of the Conscious Feminine: A New Era of Feminine Sovereignty.*

Eukharistos[21]

Philomena van Rijswijk

Crossing over the belly of the bridge
and the moon merely a wafer
held high above the mountain
like the oversized host held aloft
by the priest's tobacco-stained fingers,
while chanting the arcane mantra,
laconic as a petrol-station boy
squinting for a puncture:
Hoc est enim corpus meum...

...so deliberate, and with such authority.
The boys, in their frocks, would tinkle the bell
and we would bow our heads.
Some of the old Maltese widows would kiss Jesus
dangling from their black beads.
But, now, all of a sudden, as I mount the bridge,
I know what it was that we knelt for,
all those years ago.
It was the moon! the moon!

It was the numinous, the chickpea flour
flatbread of the moon!
Yes, we worshipped the moon,
in that dry saucer of *sorj*.

---

[21] From Gr.*eu* 'well' + *kharizesthai* 'offer graciously'.

That five-o'clock-shadowed priest
in his embroidered vestments
(cleaned and pressed by a ginger-haired
housekeeper called Mrs Judge)

worshipped the moon and her rushing, her blushing
tides, her iron-oxide inundations.
"This is my blood which will be given up for you!"
the priest would drone, oblivious to the real blood
welling up on church benches, in confessionals,
even the nuns oozing onto torn rags.
The world awash in the blood of women;
douched in the bruising and bloodying of women,
outside -in and inside -out.

And, how strangely ironic that it's him, there,
strung up on that cross, with those five raw wounds.

Author's Note: I was driving over the curve of the Tasman Bridge
one morning, and I saw the moon hanging over the city, and I
thought: "It looks like the host that the priest holds up, when he
says 'This is my body..." And, I realized that Communion is moon
worship. That led to thinking of the next thing he says: "This is my
blood, which has been given up for you..." Yes, the next thing that
happens is that the wine (blood) is consecrated. Have you ever
noticed the shape of a chalice? Not so different than Venus. In
Latin, what the priest says are these words: "Hoc est enim corpus
meum..." And that phrase is the origin of the term "hocus pocus"...
a term that is often referred to the wisdom of the crone. Hence,
my painting...

hoc
enim
corpus
meum;
hoc enim
calix
sanguinis mei

Echoes of Mesopotamia

Molly Remer

Echoes of Mesopotamia
small figures from ancient places
ancient times
and ancient faces
ancient words
and ancient wisdom
still flowing in my veins
Clay in my hands
clay in her hands
running on the rivers of time
spiraling in the mysteries of being
spinning in the eddies and ripples of eternity...

I have a strong emotional connection to ancient Paleolithic and Neolithic Goddess sculptures. I do not find that I feel as personally connected to later Goddess imagery of Greek and Roman eras. Rather, the very ancient figures are those that call to something deep and powerful within me. I have a sculpture of the Goddess of Willendorf at a central point on my altar. Sometimes I hold her and wonder and muse about who carved the original. I almost feel a thread that reaches out and continues to connect us to that nearly lost past—all the culture and society and *how very much we don't know* about early human history. There is such a solid power to these early figures and to me they speak of the numinous, non-personified, Great Goddess weaving her way throughout time and space.

What were they thinking? Those ancient women who transformed stone into potent and enduring images of the Goddess? Who crafted with their hands something that persisted for 5,000, 10,000, 15,000, 20,000, 30,000 years; images so compelling that they reach across time, space, and understanding to say hello. Who made them and what was she thinking? Who am I and what am I thinking? Perhaps it is encoded in the layers of our being. Carrying on a legacy. The next link in a chain that spans the centuries and that is beyond the reach of history.

During a women's circle session of *Rise Up and Call Her Name*, we talked about our personal cultural histories and we began work on "sacred bundles" that we continued adding to throughout the year-long course. To my beginning bundle, I added photos of my ancestors, a fossilized stone shell (because the Earth itself represents the shared cultural history of us all), and one of my own Goddess sculptures, and then I tied the bundle with a Goddess of Willendorf necklace. I surprised myself by bursting into tears when I tried to explain the significance of my items, viscerally feeling the swift swirl of time and how those grandmothers and great-grandmothers in my pictures are now *gone*, but they were people, just like me. I also shared about the deep connection I feel to the land I live on and how my parents moved here in the 1970's, so maybe this land in the Ozarks isn't really where I "come from," but *this* is where my blood and roots belong anyway. I continued crying as I described how when I sculpt my little figures, I feel like I'm part of an unbroken chain that stretches back at least 35,000 years, from the person who carved the Willendorf Goddess, all the way down to me with my rocks and clay.

Later that week, my dad said he needed to talk to me and he shared that actually in our family history it is really only he who "broke the chain" of being "from" this exact patch of the Earth, here in central Missouri. He shared that *he* was the only member of his side of the family in a long time who *wasn't* born here and that, in truth, *six generations of my family* on my paternal side were born, lived, and died within a 25 mile radius of this very hillside that I find so meaningful now. He said that he felt like his blood called him back here and he left California as a young man to return to Missouri and raise his own children here because it called him so powerfully (I was born at home one mile from where I now live). So, he said, *no wonder you feel like **this** is your cultural heritage and where you belong. Your lineage is right here, right where you like to be.*

When I was taking a Goddess history class at Ocean Seminary College, I wrote the following about the common use of red ochre on Goddess figures:

> As I saw the slideshow and reflected on Goddess figures I have known and loved, I was suddenly struck by the realization that the walls of my home are, in a sense, colored with red ochre. We live in a straw bale house and the walls are plastered with an earthen plaster that includes the red Missouri "clay dirt" that is a primary feature of the Ozarks region in which I live. The clay is red because of iron oxide, which is how red ochre is also defined. I looked at the Goddess of Willendorf on my altar and at her rich reddish color that exactly matches the shade of the earth on my bedroom walls. No wonder I feel such a deep, personal

connection to these ancient figures—quite literally, some part of me identifies Her with ***home***!

Once when I shared a photo of some of my Goddess sculptures on Facebook, someone left a comment saying simply: **Echoes of Mesopotamia.** And, I said, *exactly!*

Goddesscraft.
Womancraft.
Lifecraft.
Who molds who?
Who sculpts who?
Is it just one beautiful dance
of exuberant co-creation?
Expansive memory,
silent witness,
inner wisdom,
embodied connection
solid space
all twisted together
in an incredible tapestry
of time
culture
power
and life.

Throne for a Goddess,
Sculptural Seating

Glen Rogers

Throne for a Goddess is an interactive sculptural seat inspired by the Venus of Willendorf, one of the oldest and most celebrated Paleolithic Goddess sculptures in the world. While visiting Austria in October 2019, I was awed by seeing the Venus at close range at The Natural History Museum in Vienna. This 4.4-inch figure, exquisitely carved in stone, is almost 30,000 years old, and was discovered in Willendorf, lower Austria in 1908.

Like many women around the world, I have been inspired by this Great Mother figure as a symbol of female empowerment honoring women as life-givers. The Venus is an archetype that points to ancient Goddess cultures and matriarchal societies, which have been the focus of my artwork over many years.

The sculpture was designed at my studio in San Miguel de Allende, Mexico and fabricated at the Binder Company with Jitka Derler, another artist in the park, facilitating the work. The final sculpture is made of a combination of gold-tone anodized aluminum and steel with a rust patina. A graphic that includes the Venus figure, the moon, spirals and text are cut into the surface. It stands 6.5 feet tall by 34" wide.

I invite visitors to sit and feel the energy of the Great Mother and contemplate the inspirational message that is cut into the metal:

Rest in the Warm Embrace of the Goddess, the Great Mother, the Divine Feminine. Feel Her Nurturing Love and Offer of Abundance and Prosperity. Sit in Her Lap of Fertility and Plant a Seed for your Dreams and New Beginnings.

I am delighted to have my piece, *Throne for a Goddess,* installed at the beautiful Kunstpark St. Ruprecht/Raab. I was introduced to Wolfgang Neffe by Franz Ertl, another artist in the park, while traveling in Austria last year and made a proposal shortly after. Although I was not able to attend the September opening due to Covid travel restrictions, I look forward to seeing the Throne in person as soon as it is safe to fly.

Because I wasn't able to attend, I decided to create a commemorative print as a way to honor the project and offer something to my local community, San Miguel de Allende, Mexico. I partnered with a local non-profit, Mujeres en Cambio *since this project is all about empowering and honoring women—from the ancient to the present*. Mujeres en Cambio was a logical choice since they empower young women in rural communities by offering scholarships for their education. VP Trish Leaven said, *"these times are greatly affecting how NGO's like ours continue to raise funds to support our young women, so offers like hers (Glen's) are truly appreciated."*

The *Throne for a Goddess* commemorative print is available for $100USD with 40% going to Mujeres en Cambio. The archival, limited edition print is 11.5" x 8.5" and is signed and numbered by the artist. Order via my website: www.glenrogersart.com/shop

REST IN THE WARM
EMBRACE OF THE
GODDESS, GREAT
MOTHER, DIVINE
FEMININE. FEEL HER
NURTURING LOVE
27,500 B.C.
AND ABUNDANCE.
SIT IN HER LAP
OF FERTILITY AND
PLANT A SEED FOR
YOUR DREAMS AND
NEW BEGINNINGS.
AUSTRIA
VENUS VON WILLENDORF
THRONE FOR A GODDESS . GLEN ROGERS
ST.RUPRECHT/RAAB, AUSTRIA . SEPTEMBER 2020

We are Divine and Holy—
The Message of Goddess of Willendorf

Tamara Albanna

In writing a children's book on the Willendorf Goddess, it would appear that I have it all figured out. That I'm so comfortable in my skin, so happy in my body, I'm completely unfazed by what others may think or say, or what society expects of me with regards to my appearance.

Nothing, absolutely nothing, could be further from the truth.

I have lived in this body for 40 years, most of that time it was a love/hate relationship—with an emphasis on the hate as I got older. These days I have reconciled a lot, I can look at myself naked and not recoil. I could even undress in front of a lover and not worry about what they might think.

But sometimes, it creeps up on me. A snide comment here, a funny look there—and it all comes crashing down.

I have accepted that this very well may be a lifelong struggle. That I will possibly never be completely happy in this body—and I have to be perfectly OK with that, because, I'm not perfect.

I have learned that as a woman of Middle Eastern descent, I am simply not supposed to look like what the Western media pushes on us as an ideal. I understand that as a mother, the "price" I paid for literally creating life, is a softer belly and stretch marks. I also appreciate that there is literally no one like me, or like you. That's what makes us beautiful, it is our uniqueness, like I say in our beautiful Willendorf children's book.

To young girls, especially... I just want to remind you that you are absolutely amazing and incredible just as you are. Just because you exist, because you are YOU. Please don't ever let anyone tell you otherwise or make you feel any less than the magnificence of what you are. The story I tell in this book—the message this wondrous Goddess is giving us—is that we are all worthy, as we are. There is nothing to "fix"—there are no mistakes—you really are Divine, and whole.

I wanted to be open and honest, I didn't want anyone to pick up this book and assume that I somehow have it all together—I really don't.

I also want you to know that it's OK if you don't have it together too. Let us embrace ourselves the best way we know how, and be kind to our precious bodies. They deserve at least that much.

The Girl God Meets
Goddess of Willendorf

Trista Hendren

My daughter, Helani Claire, who inspired *The Girl God* book,
in Vienna with myself and Auntie Tamara Albanna in January of 2018.

On Raising Daughters to Love Themselves

Trista Hendren

Toward the end of my undergraduate degree, I took a class on Women and Fat through the Women's Studies department at Portland State University. We studied texts such as *Fat is a Feminist Issue*—and ended the term with our own projects. I remember mine was called *The Fat in My Family*. I wish I had saved it so I could see what my 21-year-old-self wrote, but I also know it would probably break my heart.

Fat has always been something that has been at the forefront of my mind. I remember one of my sisters went through a phase where she measured her entire body with a tape measure (waist, thighs, arms) and weighed herself daily. I too spent a lot of time terrified of becoming 'fat'—as if that was the *worst* fate on the planet.

Some years ago, that same sister recommended that I read Anita A. Johnston's *Eating in the Light of the Moon*—which baffled me. I did not see myself as having a problem. It took years for me to finally sit down and read it. It is a groundbreaking book and was transformative in my healing process. In it, Johnson asks:

> "Why has a naturally masculine shape (broad shoulders, no waist, narrow hips, flat belly) become the ideal for the female body? Why is it that those aspects of a woman's body that are most closely related to her innate female power, the capacity of her belly, hips, and thighs to carry and sus-

tain life, are diminished in our society's version of a beautiful woman?"[22]

I realized that I had been so terrified of being deemed 'fat,' that I had reached my fourth decade without any sense of how much I actually needed to eat. I had somehow infantilized myself—despite that fact that I felt I had taken back my power and independence through feminism over the last two decades. As Naomi Wolf wrote:

> "A culture fixated on female thinness is not an obsession about female beauty, but an obsession about female obedience. Dieting is the most potent political sedative in women's history; a quietly mad population is a tractable one."[23]

I have fought too hard to divorce myself from soul-crushing patriarchal teachings to be caged by any sort of diet. And while I have prided myself on never dieting, the truth is that I have always been afraid to eat 'too much.'

I think so many of us are raised as girls not to take up space or be too full of ourselves. I have to wonder how much of this also collides with our sexuality and financial abundance. As Linda Reuther noted:

> "When I first saw the Venus of Willendorf many years ago, I was frightened by her fullness. In our society, we get the message that that kind of abundance is absolutely

---

[22] Johnston PhD, Anita A. *Eating in the Light of the Moon: How Women Can Transform Their Relationship with Food Through Myths, Metaphors, and Storytelling.* Gurze Books; 2000.
[23] Wolf, Naomi, *The Beauty Myth: How Images of Beauty Are Used Against Women.* Harper Perennial; 2002.

unacceptable. It took me awhile to embrace her. As the archetypal Great Mother, this incredibly abundant and revered woman often makes people uncomfortable. She is so large, sensual, voluptuous and ripe with the fertility of feminine energy and power. Our discomfort with her is a reflection of how we are raised as women-what size we are taught is acceptable and what is not acceptable."[24]

I wanted to publish this book on my 46th birthday because it has been important and cathartic work for me. A few days before the scheduled publication date, I did not want to get out of bed—which is very unlike me. The start of this year has been grueling in every way. It has been disappointing because I had so hoped for a better year after the shit show of 2020. But absolutely nothing has gone right this year from the moment I woke up New Year's Day. Full-on Trista style, I have forged through anyway at full speed.

But 3 days before publication, I had no energy. I stayed in bed a few hours and meditated, hugged myself, and slept on and off. I got up to go to the bathroom, let the dog out and made sure my daughter was on her way to school. I decided to go back to bed and read, returning to Christiane Northrup's *Women's Bodies, Women's Wisdom*—lingering on her *Inner Child Rescue Meditation*.[25] After working my way through that, I had enough energy to get up and start my day, albeit 3 hours late. One of my first tasks was to read a chapter from my new friend Kay Louise Aldred's upcoming book, *Re-Membering with Goddess: Healing the Patriarchal Perpetuation*

---

[24] Reuther, Linda. *Her words: An Anthology of Poetry about the Great Goddess,* Edited by Burleigh Muten. Shambhala; 1st edition, 1999.
[25] Northrup, Christiane M.D. Women's Bodies, Women's Wisdom: Creating Physical and Emotional Health and Healing. Bantam; Revised edition, 2020.

of Trauma. I wrote her back immediately, venting:

> *I feel, this year especially, that so much stuff has come to the surface for me, that I actually thought I had dealt with. Ugh! I think there is SO much unprocessed trauma both individually and collectively in women. And honestly I think there is a double whammy because we do so much for everyone else that it is almost impossible to heal it or even feel it until we are practically dead. I had a tumor 4 years ago that almost killed me and I STILL do not do all the things I know I need to do to thrive every day. I'm getting better but I am still SO frustrated with myself about that.*

I pushed on through my day, realizing around 2pm that I had forgotten to eat lunch. And then, it hit me—and I burst into tears. My body was taken from me as a child by an adult who was supposed to care for me. I still don't know how to nurture her. Until I learn that, almost nothing I tell my daughter will matter. She has grown up seeing me carrying on my abuse—by my own hands. What my daughter needs most from me—aside from nurturance and protection—is to see me love and nurture myself. In my mess of tears, I asked myself: *Why is it so hard for me to love myself?*

I don't think I am the only woman who has asked herself this question. What I had committed to doing is creating a different world for my daughter. It feels impossible and hopeless to think that she may be oppressed and abused in many of the same ways I have been over the course of my life. Somehow along the way, I put my obsession over that above taking care of myself. But I need to find a balance if I really want a change.

I have worked very hard to raise my daughter in a home where she is protected from all forms of abuse—and fat is not feared. And yet, I can hear her talking with her friends and see that the world has still done a number on them.

We live in Norway, where teen magazines aren't really a thing—and advertisers are required to state when something has been photoshopped. I think there is a healthier relationship to weight here than what I am used to in the United States—but the struggle is still there. There is still a whole lot of body hatred.

Our home is filled with Goddess affirming art—including a life-size Willendorf magnet on our refrigerator. She is there for me—and She is there for all the women and girls who visit our home. The paintings of Kat Shaw, Arna Baartz, Elisabeth Slettnes and so many others have been tremendously affirming. We also put out a children's book on Willendorf last year with hopes that girls around the world would see themselves in Her image.

Photo by Alyscia Cunningham

I *still* must be careful not make degrading remarks about myself or my own weight. And if I am honest, these comments do slip out. We have all been thoroughly brainwashed to hate ourselves and our female bodies—but I do not want to carry on this tradition. My daughter watches how I treat myself, and how I talk to myself. I will set the tone for how she relates to her body.

Learning to love ourselves is often a process. I claim that love by caring deeply for my body—eating and drinking nourishing foods and juices, a daily body scrub and self-massage—and by walking, doing yoga and Qi Gong. And, by making sure I get lots of blissful sleep and orgasms. There is still a lot more I can do to spoil myself.

May our nieces, daughters, and granddaughters have an easier time with it all. May they grow up to love the curves that are WOMAN— and connect with their GODDESS essence.

My First Look at Her

Trista Hendren

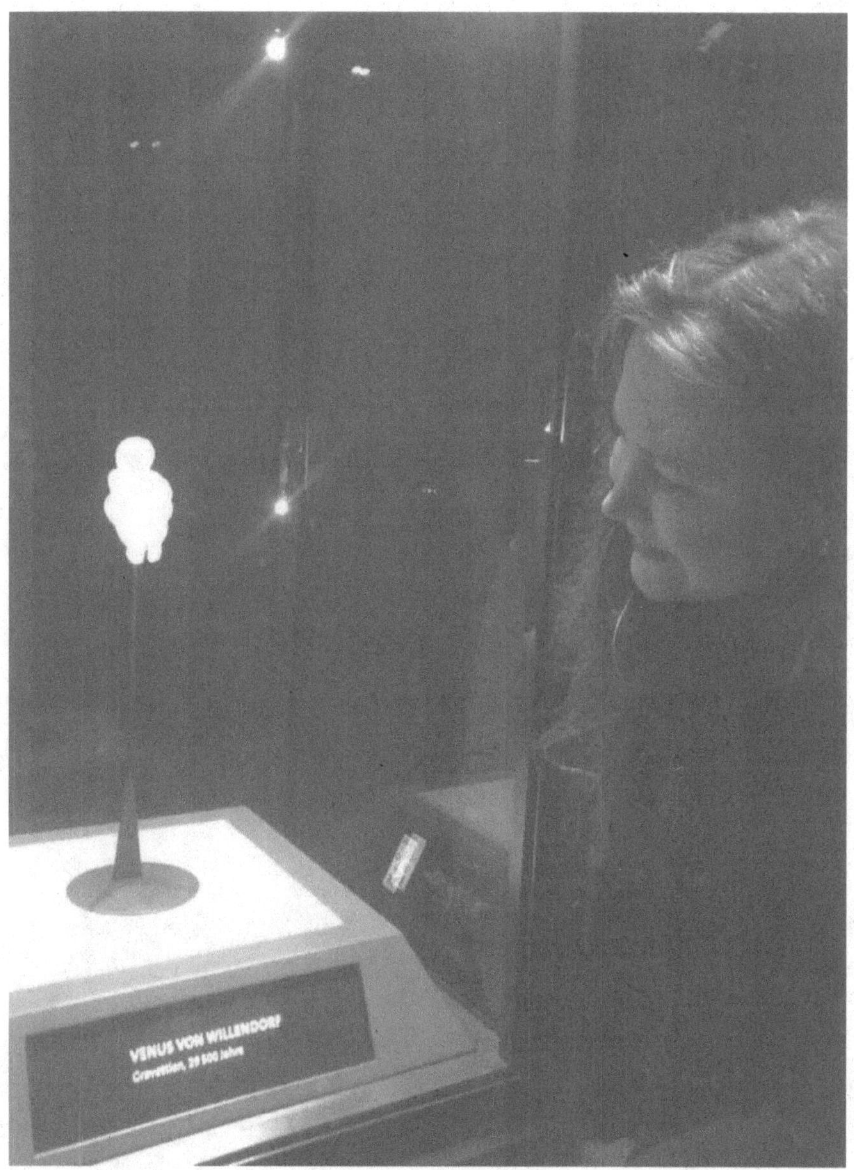

Vienna, January 2018. Photo by Tamara Albanna.

I Love You, Sweet Willendorf

Sharon Smith

Goddess of Willendorf,
Your round body called to me:
Belly roll and full, sagging breasts
"Thick thighs" and dimpled knees
Wide hips and broad, unapologetic behind.

They spoke to me in ways
No "Father God" could ever do;
They called me out of the shame
Of not having "the perfect body"
That Patriarchal men long ago defined

I love you, Sweet Willendorf!
You've broken the lock on my cage door
And set me free so that I can explore
The glorious curves of my own Goddess Body
And love my own sagging belly and drooping "shelf"

And dimpled knees and "thunder thighs."
I honor You, Sweet Willendorf,
Because you've opened up my eyes
so I can see: No Barbie Doll image could ever be
More beautiful than your ripe, succulent Self!

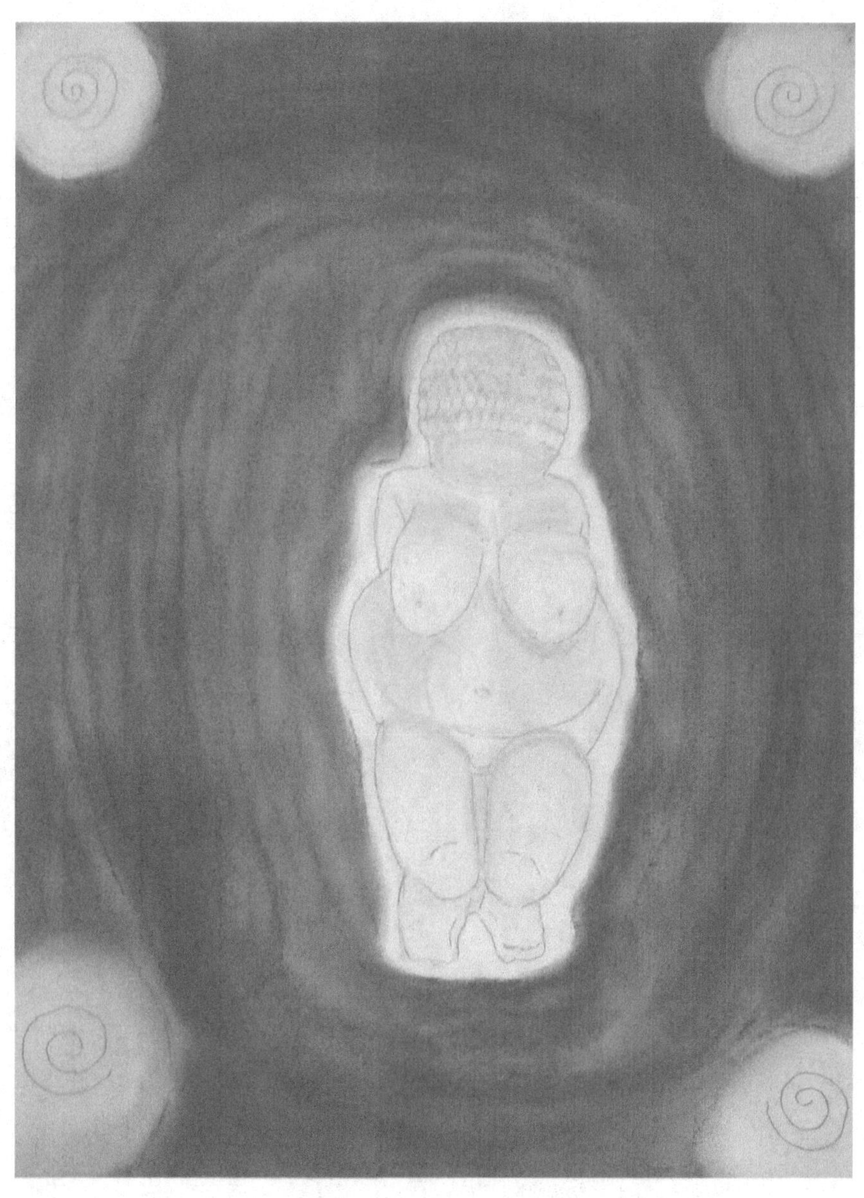

Painting by Sharon Smith

Creating MY Willendorf

Arlene Bailey

If I look at the artifact named Willendorf purely from an anthropological perspective, I have a lot of curiosity around the many references to mother, Goddess, comfort, love and acceptance. I wonder why, as modern women, we project these particular attributes onto a Paleolithic (or even earlier) artifact when in reality we have no idea who this figure represented or what she meant to the people of her time.

So what is it about her that elicits our need to afford a clay figure from thousands of years ago, all these different attributes that may or may not be true?

Is it because as modern day women we crave a symbol, some proof, that at one point in human evolution women were seen as sacred and mattered enough for someone to hand carve an image of the women of that day?

Is it because we desperately want a voluptuous symbol of the great mother whose lap and breasts are sufficient to hold and sustain us... to love and comfort us?

Perhaps it is because as modern women, we have grown exasperated and weary of the male ideal of how a woman should look and Willendorf gives us both memories and hope of another way. Perhaps we need to know that at one point in the male dominated narrative of humans, nubile was not seen as the desired way of being—but rather She of succulent breasts, round belly and full thighs. Perhaps we need to know that woman in her fullness of all things was not only wanted but desired and honored.

Carving this figure from limestone with the tools of the time would have been a timely undertaking, requiring great skill, so are we reaching back through ancestral hands and minds to be able to touch and hold the thoughts and ideas, ways and rituals of an older way?

Do we need to hold an ancient idea of woman as sacrosanct to make sense of the ideas around women in our time?

I have no answers for the truth of the *why* is lost to time. All I have are my own ideas, but they are not answers from a scholarly perspective, only those of a woman of today. For me, this hand-carved vessel which holds the memories of a different time—this image of woman in her sacred fullness of body—is a representation of a culture deeply respectful of women and one that afforded them a high level of sacredness sufficient to be immortalized in stone. Further, there had to have been an appreciation of the earth and her gifts of dirt, clay, stone, bones from animals, etc., as those items would have been needed in order to allow the creation of such a piece.

So many conversations we could have, so many ideas and theories to debate and question—and, in the end, so many unknowns when all is said and done.

Perhaps it is only how she makes each of us feel that truly matters... only our *personal* naming and honoring of her that is important...

only that our awareness encompass the knowing that even today Willendorf's legacy of a body Round and Full, Sacred and Beautiful calls to us from a timeline reaching back to 30,000 BCE.

Is it really that simple?

For me, yes.

For even though scholars will tell us Willendorf *was* this or that, but *not* this or that and others will have their own opinions, it is up to each of us to go within and gather our own sacred materials to hand carve the Willendorf that fits our hearts, minds and sacred intuitive knowing.

We must each create our own Willendorf.

Creating MY Willendorf by Arlene Bailey, ©2020

Yes All Women

Joey Hartmann-Dow

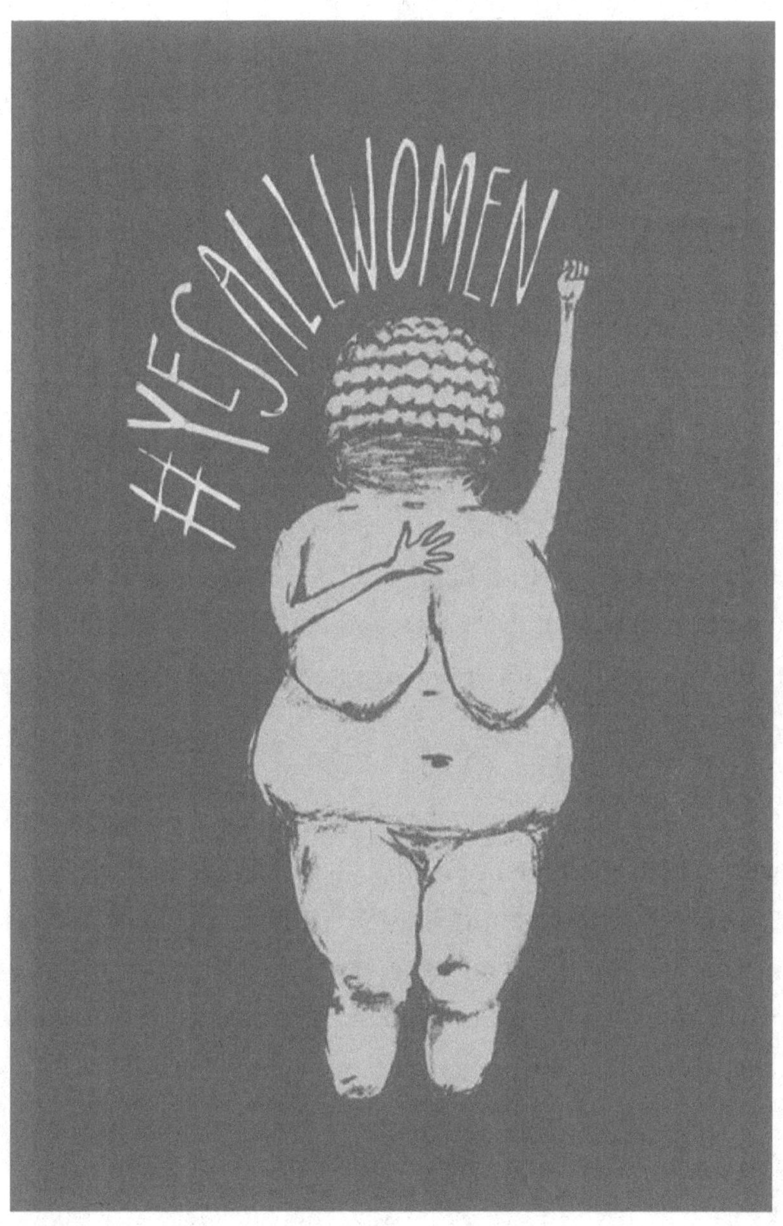

How I Learned to Love My Body:
Finding the Goddess in Sagging Boobs,
a Belly Roll and Wrinkles

Sharon Smith

Like so many girls and women, I grew up with body issues, and most of my life, I found fault with my body. I had inherited a short "chunky monkey" body that put on weight easily and refused to shed the pounds whenever I tried to diet. My life was the typical rollercoaster of gaining and losing weight, especially after I had my daughters. And my husband, at the time, didn't make my life any easier with the "Fat Albert" jokes he aimed my way.

My thighs were always "thick," my boobs too big, my butt too wide. I never considered myself "pretty" at all by societal standards and, Goddess knows, I bought the skin creams and make-up and clothing whenever I could afford them to make myself "more presentable" and "more acceptable."

But nothing ever made me feel "pretty enough" or "acceptable enough," so I fell in and out of depression on a regular basis—and being "married" (I found out quickly that a piece of paper doesn't mean a damned thing) to a man who pretty much ignored me on a daily basis, except for a few times when he wanted a quick, "wham, bam, thank you, ma'am"—which certainly didn't help.

Like so many other women suffering from a negative body image, I found solace in food: Junk food mostly, and chocolate especially. I could down one of those large Hershey's bars in a matter of moments. Or eat a pint of Ben & Jerry's New York Super Fudge Chunk in a single sitting. So, of course, I put on more weight. And the more weight I gained, the more depressed I became. And the more depressed I became, the more I self-medicated with food.

See the horrible and unhealthy cycle here? All because I had bought into a system that made women think that they needed the "approval" and "acceptance" of a man to be whole, to be worth something.

At one point in my life, when I was twenty-nine years old, I became obsessed with exercising. I added dieting to this regimen and began to lose weight. I was over 200 lbs at the time—a lot of weight on a 5'4" frame—and it was really affecting my health. So, I determined I would eat healthy—which meant only salads with "diet dressings" and diet sodas and drinks containing aspartame, the new "non-sugar sweetener." I lifted weights three times a week for an hour each time; I did two hours of spot exercises each day (an hour in the morning and an hour before bedtime), and I jogged 14 miles a day (seven miles in the morning and seven miles in the late afternoon—each session measuring 37 laps around our high school's track). To say I was an exercise-a-holic is putting it mildly.

And yes, I lost weight. I got "buff" and men started noticing me. I dropped to around 110 pounds. I got whistled at when I wore my one-piece bathing suit to the lake or the beach. Guys slowed their cars and asked me if I wanted a ride as I walked down the street. But I wasn't stupid. I knew what they were "interested in." Besides, I was a married woman, and a Christian at the time, so I was bound by my faith to be a "good, submissive wife," even though my husband felt no compulsion to "love" me "as Christ loved the Church."

All of my weight loss wasn't simply for health reasons; much of it was to gain my husband's love and approval. I thought if I took care of myself better and got thin, he would notice me and be proud of me. Sad to say, that was not the case. He didn't seem to notice me any more in my "thin, buff body" than he did in my "Fat Albert" one.

So, yes, eventually the depression took hold again, and I started putting the weight back on.

That unhealthy cycle didn't begin to change until I discovered my husband had been cheating on me with a woman from his workplace. But I had to look death squarely in the face before I got my first real epiphany about my life.

When I knew beyond a shadow of a doubt that my husband was sleeping with another woman, I went to a group of elder women in my church for support and help. I was horribly disappointed when they told me flat out, "You CAN'T leave your husband! God HATES divorce. You must be doing something wrong if your husband feels the need to look outside the home for attention. You need to go home and work harder at being a more submissive wife!"

Those words cut deep. No support at all. I walked out of that "counseling session" feeling like the entire weight of the world was on my shoulders. No fault given to my husband. It was obviously ALL MY FAULT. And I had worked so damned hard to try to make that man feel like "the King of his Castle" as we ladies were taught in women's group. What else could I do?

That evening, while washing dishes at the kitchen sink, I picked up a carving knife and thought about slitting my wrists right then and there; how easy it would be to "end it all." "If THIS is the best you have for me, God, then I don't want it!" I said aloud. I already hated myself for being fat; now I was told by women I had respected highly that I was incompetent too.

Thank the Goddess, I didn't go through with it. My love for my two daughters kept me from harming myself. I didn't want to leave them with a "father" who showed as little interest in them as he did in me. I just couldn't do that to them.

So, in that moment, I cried out to the Universe for iron to enter my soul. I needed a backbone for what I was about to do next: kick my cheating, abusive, neglectful husband's ass out the door!

My story of "My Body, Myself" began to change the moment I sent that man packing. He tried for two years to keep me on a leash but I finally divorced him; and the moment the papers arrived, you can bet I celebrated.

I eventually married my second husband, a Vietnam veteran with PTSD—and you might be thinking, "What the hell? How could THAT be better?" But it was. Because Jerry loved me no matter my body shape or size, and he taught me how to be a strong woman. He said he didn't want a "mousey, submissive woman"—what he needed was a "Kick-Ass Woman" in his life. And so I gradually became one.

And I eventually escaped from fundamentalist Christianity—the patriarchal religion that had ruled most of my adult life up to that point.

After my beloved husband passed in April of 2010 from the debilitating effects of Agent Orange, I began my real journey of self-discovery and, more important, of learning to love myself. I was in my mid-50s by then. (Better late than never, right?) I began to immerse myself in Women's Studies and to learn about the Patriarchy and how it has negatively impacted both women and men. The whole body issue problem with girls and women is directly connected to this misogynistic system and its unholy teachings.

Needing a change, this East Coast Girl moved out to the Pacific Northwest in September of 2012, eventually settling in a little community in NE Washington state, where I became involved in women's retreats twice a year at a lovely mountaintop retreat center, and began to connect with like-minded Sisters. I discovered at these retreats how many women share the same wounds—and a LOT of them are connected to body image: We're too skinny; we're too fat, we're not pretty enough, etc., etc., etc. And that further revealed to me the insidious ways in which Patriarchy has fed into the female psyche that we HAVE to fit man's criteria for "beauty" or we're just not worth the effort.

That's when I learned to say, "FUCK THAT SHIT!" and I started to look at myself, and my aging Crone Body in a new light... which is actually a very OLD light, really: The way we women saw ourselves and were seen by men BEFORE Patriarchy flipped the story and forced us to live in their hellish "reality."

I began to look at my naked body, with its drooping "baby roll," sagging breasts, cellulite thighs and wrinkles; its growing waddle under my chin and its greying hair… and to smile and say, "My Goddess, you're BEAUTIFUL!" And (the Big One): "I LOVE YOU just as you are!" To be honest, THAT was a journey in itself, because you don't undo years and years of patriarchal conditioning in one day, or even one month… But you CAN undo it.

What helped me so much—and I can't stress this enough—is joining a women's group and having a safe place in which to share, without criticism or condemnation of any kind, your story. To shed your tears. To scream it out if necessary and have the loving arms of your Sisters holding you in that Sacred Space. If you don't have such a group or a circle, I lovingly suggest you find one and become a regular part of it. Sisters, we NEED each other. There is a saying, "We rise by lifting each other up" and that is so true for us, as women. Patriarchy still exists, and many of our Sisters are still trapped in it, struggling under it. And some are trapped in it, but like songbirds in a gilded cage, they know nothing else BUT the cage and are content to stay in it. Both need to be freed.

Within Patriarchy, it is very difficult to find our sovereignty as women, and it is through our sovereignty that we can embrace our bodies as they are—and celebrate them, as they are, without feeling a sense of "shame" or "disgust." And that is why I encourage all my Sisters to escape from the system, so together, we can create a better way.

Our bodies are Divine. Our bodies are Sacred. We represent the Great Mother, whose full-bodied shape was chiseled in stone, forged in metal, carved in wood, and honored for hundreds of thousands of years before Patriarchy reared its ugly head. Let's not forget that.

One of my favorite Goddess figurines is the Goddess of Willendorf. She is a short, well-rounded little Goddess with big, sagging boobs, a large round belly, thick thighs and a big behind. Whenever I see Her, I am flooded with such a sense of Love and gratitude, because She was the Goddess who finally broke the Patriarchal lock on my mind and opened the door wide to my own Goddess-body. And for that, I am eternally thankful!

May you discover your own beautiful, glorious Goddess-body, my Sisters! You need do nothing to change that body. She is your Temple, and She is perfect as She is! Give Her some love today, won't you?

[NOTE: Re: "You need do nothing to change that body." If you desire to lose weight at any time for YOURSELF (for health reasons, for instance) then do it. I am not advocating living in any unhealthy situation. However, there are many healthy, full-bodied women who really don't need to lose weight. They have embraced their Goddess-bodies as they are. I am honored to know a number of these wonderful full-bodied Sisters who are belly dancers here in North Carolina where I presently live. They inspire me daily with their gracefulness and their beauty. They truly are Goddesses in my book! And that is what I am talking about here.]

Decolonize Body Love

Amber Quinonez

© NagolaBodyPositive. Prints and t-shirts available
on the NagolaBodyPositive shop on Etsy.

Take Cover Girl

Luisah Teish

Beauty not brought to you by Cover Girl.

It is definitely time to uncover,
The way we have to function undercover,
While uncovering the deceptions of this culture
That covers up who we really are.

I really want to invite sisters to
Throw back the covers,
To WAKE UP,
GET UP,
STAND UP.

I want us to
STEP Down,
JUMP OFF,
FLY AWAY,
From the crazy Cover Girl concept of Beauty
That has actually acted as a way to enact some acts of violence
against our beautiful BE-INGS.

We be beautiful sisters!
With our nappy heads full of brilliant ideas.
We be beautiful sisters!
With our rhythm beating Bantu behinds.
We be beautiful sisters!

With our straight-talking hot tongues wagging
All the goddamn time.

We be beautiful sisters.
We be beautiful sisters.
We be beautiful everywhere we be.
We be beautiful
And we COVER THE WORLD
GIRL.

Luisah Teish for Emi Okun Feb. 2013

Living Goddess

Alyscia Cunningham

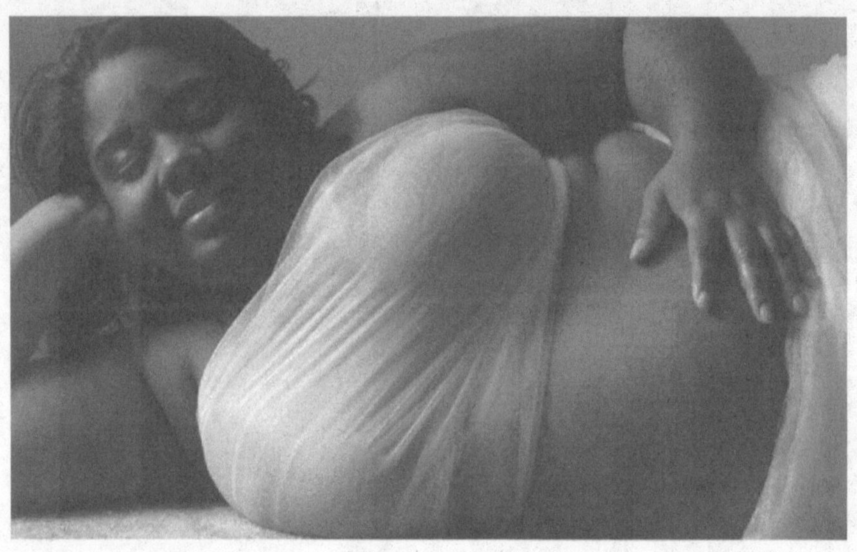

The Palm of My Hand
Molly Remer

"If there is one chant in the universe it is to *create*."
–Chris Griscolm quoted in *Nicole Christine*, p. 25

If you ever eavesdrop on a conversation between my husband and me around the clamor of our four children's voices, you will probably hear me making a tired lament: "All I want is a broad swath of uninterrupted *time*." In listening to Elizabeth Gilbert's newest book, *Big Magic*, on audio book, I was interested by her mention that many creative people lament not having long stretches of uninterrupted *time* available in which to work. She quotes a letter from Herman Melville to Nathaniel Hawthorne, lamenting his lack of time and how he is always pulled "hither and thither by circumstances." Melville said that he longed for a wide-open stretch of time in which to write. She says he called it, "the calm, the coolness, the silent grass-growing mood in which a man ought always to compose."

> ...I do not know of any artist (successful or unsuccessful, amateur or pro) who does not long for that kind of time. I do not know of any creative soul who does not dream of calm, cool, grass-growing days in which to work without interruption. Somehow, though, nobody ever seems to achieve it. Or if they do achieve it (through a grant, for instance, or a friend's generosity, or an artist's residency), that idyll is just temporary—and then life will inevitably rush back in. Even the most successful creative people I know complain that they never seem to get all the hours they

need in order to engage in dreamy, pressure-free, creative exploration. Reality's demands are constantly pounding on the door and disturbing them. On some other planet, in some other lifetime, perhaps that sort of peaceful Edenic work environment does exist, but it rarely exists here on earth. Melville never got that kind of environment, for instance. But he still somehow managed to write *Moby-Dick*, anyhow.[26]

When I create a new sculpture, I am most often creating something that I need to *remember* or want to *learn*. The original figures for

---

[26] Elizabeth Gilbert *On Unlocking Creativity, Ideas As Viruses.* News | OPB.

my *Centered Mama* sculpture and my *Meditation Goddess* sculpture were both created while at a friend's house for a weekend work exchange as my baby toddled around. While I love making figures of mothers and babies, I was feeling a strong urge to make a Goddess representation *complete unto herself.* A Goddess who embodied wholeness, as she is, on her own, like the Goddess of Willendorf—self-sovereign, powerful and whole. It felt like a reclaiming of my non-maternal identity and a declaration of self-sovereignty to work on non-maternal Goddess sculptures. My original Meditation Goddess turned out to be a little bigger than some of my other figures, strong and secure and independent. Then, the baby crawled over and knocked off one of her breasts, knocked her over on the tray, smashing the side of her head. I came close to crying. I felt annoyed with my husband who'd "let" him come over and destroy my work rather than noticing him doing it and stopping him. I was frustrated, dismayed, and my feelings felt hurt. First I felt like, *Argh! This is a metaphor for life!* And, then I realized it was not just a *metaphor* for life, it *is* my actual life! I pouted a bit and said I was just going to smash her and give up and I made some bitter faces at my husband and some long-suffering huffs and signs, but then the baby fell asleep in the Ergo, held close against my chest. I kissed his soft hair and I took my clay and started again.

I reclaimed her from the smashed parts and she sat stronger and taller than ever. She reminds me not to give up and that beautiful work can come from struggle, but also of *interdependence* (not just the independence I was going for!), co-creation, and tenacity. When the finished version of her, cast from the original sculpt, sits by my bed at night or overlooks my dinner preparations, she reminds me that I am strong and that persistence is worthwhile. She also *tries* to remind me to be calm and steady, centered and Zen, even though I more often feel like a whirlwind.

That same Saturday at my friend's house, as my baby tentatively toddled around the kitchen, chewed on a piece of watermelon, and snoozed on my chest, I felt moved to begin creating a new Centered Mama sculpture. I had been going through an emotional rough patch, feeling buffeted by variable emotions and was erratic and unpredictable in my enthusiasm and confidence. I was also feeling impatient, snappy, and irritable.

> *"I will be gentle with myself.*
> *I will be tender with my heart.*
> *I will hold my heart like a newborn baby child."*

This song by Karen Drucker replayed in my mind as I sculpted. The baby woke, the watermelon got dragged along the floor collecting dust, and it was time for our collaborative dinner, so I had to put her away unfinished. When we got back to our own home, I was compelled to *finish* her, working feverishly as the baby pulled on my legs and I said, "just a few more minutes!" to the older kids who were trying to play with him to let me work. Again and again I re-rolled the clay baby's head, trying to make it "perfect," and worked to lay down the strands of her hair, against the backdrop of this often-chaotic, noisy, home-based life we've consciously and intentionally created together. She was created to represent holding my own center in the midst of motherhood. *I will be tender with my heart.* I don't create sculptures like this because I *AM* so

"Zen" and have life all figured out, I make them to remind me what is possible if I listen to my soul.

As I made slow progress on my dissertation, an exploration of contemporary priestessing in the United States, I typed a quote from the book *Priestess: Woman as Sacred Celebrant* by Pamela Eakins, about her past life memories of making clay Goddess figures as a temple priestess:

> "…to me it brought a continuation of the energy of the sacred objects of the grandmothers. I contained this energy in a new form in the dolls that would be placed upon the altars and in the graves of the daughters living now and the daughters to come…
>
> I felt this process made my own clay stronger, too. Some of the pieces cracked in the fire because of the added 'impurities'…but, in this case, I felt the impurities were the purest of pure and I worshipped each crack knowing the crack contained the wisdom of the priestesses who had occupied the doll-making table for more moons than I could even imagine. It contained too, the devotional energy of every grandmother who had held it in her hands or placed it on her altar. Sometimes 'impurities' sanctify further that which is holy to begin with."

While I tend to have a knee-jerk skepticism about past-life memories, there is something in Eakins' words that I know at a bone-deep level as I do my own work with Goddesscraft:

"...Each Goddess was imprinted with the sound of sacred life coursing through the Universe. I changed with the priestesses as the figures came through my hands. Each doll received the sacred vibration of life... For seventy-seven moons I made the dolls at the long table with the young Sisters of Nun. My hands were so fast. I made thousands of figures: beautiful little faces, etched collars of gold plates, pubic hair swirled into tiny rows of connecting spirals. They were so precious. At the end of the day, my baked clay shelves were covered with little women.

The clay Goddesses healed...

This is how I apprenticed. I learned, in this manner, the art of healing. I learned that to heal means to make whole, and that becoming whole involves learning many levels of purification, balance, and reformation." (p. 32-33).

In Anne Key's marvelous priestess memoir, *Desert Priestess*, she makes this important point: "It is of course no small wonder why graven images are so tightly controlled by religious traditions." (p. 52) Sometimes I feel like this is what I'm tapping into when I make my own Goddess sculptures—a resistance to tight control over graven images and over personalization of divinity as male.

I occasionally get requests to make bigger Goddesses—people ask about figures that are large altar pieces 12-18 inches tall or taller. The Goddesses I make are all under four inches tall and there's a reason for that: *they fit in the palm of my hand*. When I create them, I feel as if I'm part of an unbroken lineage stretching back 30,000 years to the person who carved the Goddess of Willendorf. I feel connected to the priestesses of the Mesopotamian temples who sculpted hundreds upon hundreds of tiny clay Goddesses. Someone commented on my sculptures once saying, "echoes of Mesopotamia." And, I said, "*exactly*." I feel the connection between the clay in my hand and the clay in their hands, running through the ripples and eddies of time.

In Starhawk's *The Spiral Dance*, she writes of the attempts to discredit Goddess religion by invalidating the historical narratives or archaeological evidence: "The idea seems to be that if they can disprove our origin story, they can invalidate our spirituality... Is Buddhism invalid if we cannot find archaeological evidence of Buddha's existence? Are Christ's teachings unimportant if we cannot find his birth certificate or death warrant? ...the truth of our experience is valid whether it has roots thousands of years old or thirty minutes old... a mythic truth whose proof is shown not through references and footnotes but in the way it engages strong emotions, mobilizes deep life energies, and gives us a sense of history, purpose, and place in the world. What gives the Goddess tradition validity is how it works for us now, in the moment, not whether or not someone else worshiped this particular image in the past." (p. 4).

The ancestry of my Goddess sculptures may not be the same energy that raised temples and built monuments (or walls), it is the energy that carried a baby on one hip and a basket of supplies on the other and needed a Goddess just the right size to tuck down the front of a shirt...

Sometimes I describe my life in the woods as being held in the hand of the Goddess. And, I make Goddesses that I hold in my hand. Am I in the palm of Her hand or is She in the palm of mine?

The answer is *both*.

In Her Hands

Arna Baartz

Shedding Skins
Anique Radiant Heart

I can't remember when I first started to hate my body... at age 73, my memory is not all that good. I think it may have been when I went to school, and I looked different than most of the other girls. Not only because I was poor and my second-hand uniform was just that little bit faded, but also because I was fatter than the rest. It took years and years, a marriage and 2 kids to finally (at age 28) decide that I needed to love my body. This came as a realization as my feminist sensibilities began to grow and I met women of all shapes and sizes who seemed to really love themselves.

By the time I was 40, I accepted my body and began to love it. I wanted to celebrate that, so I asked some of my friends to help me make a plaster cast of my body, in ritual, as a way of really "owning" myself. It was a wonderful weekend... so much laughter—as, for example, they shaved the back of my legs right up close to my bottom, and had to tape glad wrap over my yoni hairs so they would not stick... ouch! They decided that they would all be naked too, so I would not feel too exposed.

Ahhhh... the sisterhood. One thing I remember was the feeling as the plaster dried and it lifted off my skin. I imagined I was a snake and I was shedding my old skin. It was liberating. Over the years, my Venus has been with me to many Goddess conferences around Australia. And She has graced many altars in my homes and Temples over the years. I love Her and now I love my body too, unreservedly.

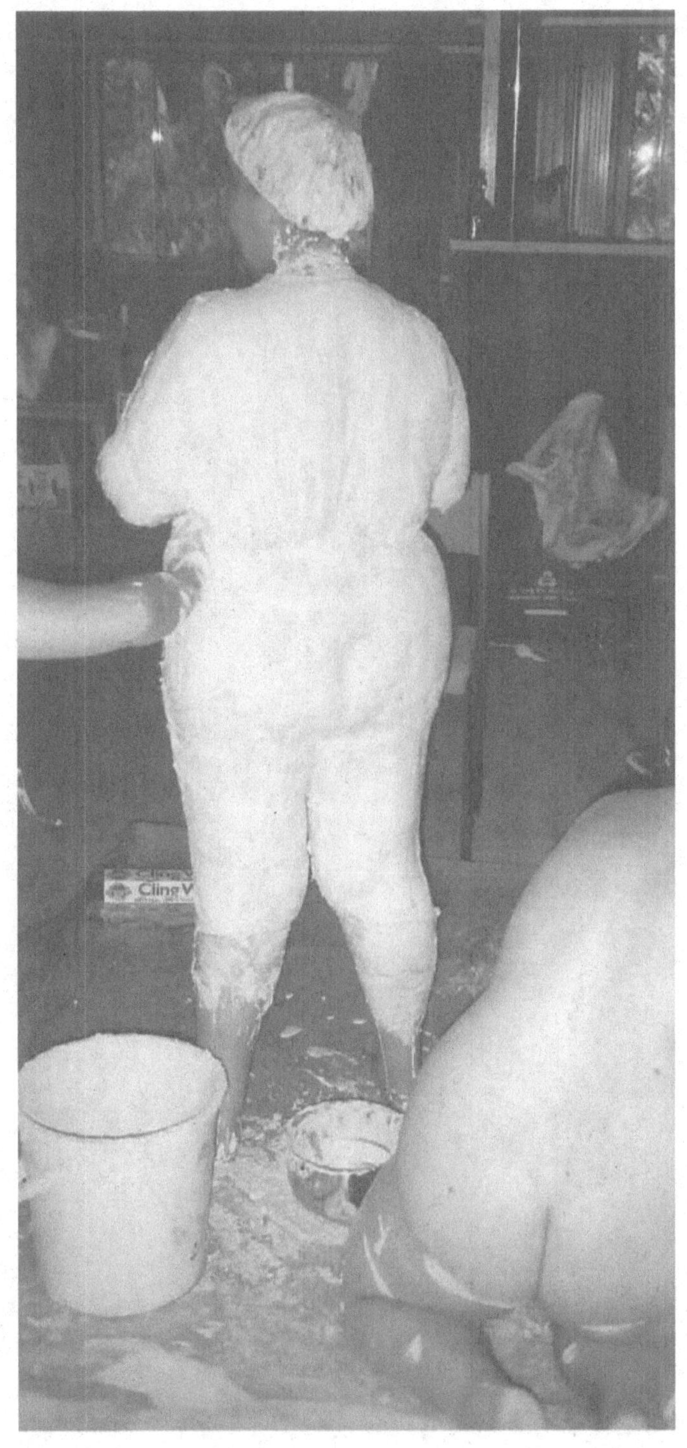

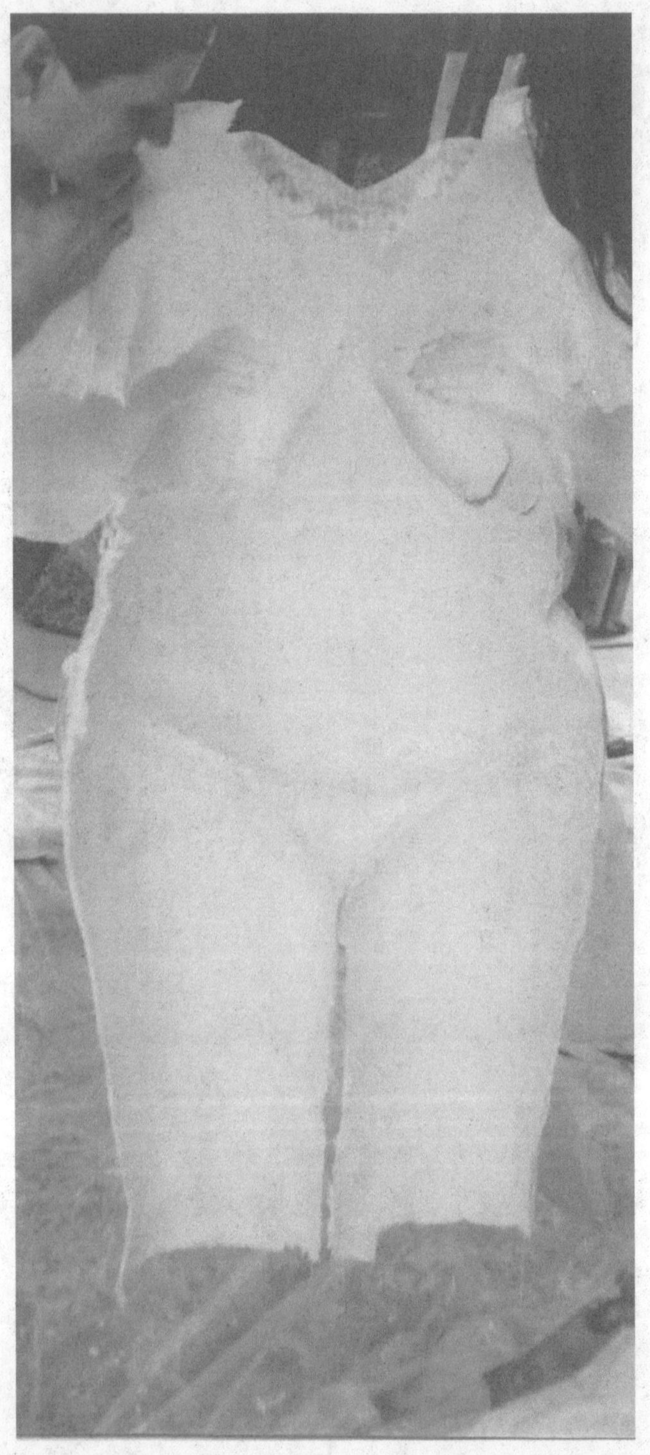

Survivors – And Still I Rise

Kat Shaw

"We will not let the past define our lives.
We will show the world that surviving can be beautiful.
We are here, living, despite it all.
Reclaiming our strength.
Reawakening our Inner Goddess.
Reassociating with our bodies.
We will always rise, and we will do so with strength and dignity.
We bow down to the universe who is proud of who we are.
We are the magical souls whose spirits cannot be broken and
whose strength cannot be questioned.
We are the survivors."

Survivors is an ongoing art project by Kat Shaw, to empower and celebrate glorious women who have survived and used the broken pieces of their lives to build a bridge and walk forward with strength and power. Our bodies have to withstand a lot – physically, emotionally, mentally and medically, and this can leave visible or invisible scars – which can be regarded by society as unsightly. And as Kat is always pushing back against society's perception of perfection and creating a new way for women to love themselves, defining their own beauty – this project, inspired by the poem by Maya Angelou, was the perfect accolade to be exhibited on International Women's Day 2020 at Goddess House in Glastonbury.

These ladies bodies tell their glorious tales, and there is such power in that. The determination and spirit it has taken them to fight another day – supported by their glorious flesh.

So far in the project, Kat has painted 135 women who have survived. Each painting has the words "And still I rise" written directly onto them, and their strapline is written and overlaid on acetate, so it can be peeled back by the survivors and released.

What they had survived is their story, but not their ending.
And still, they rise.

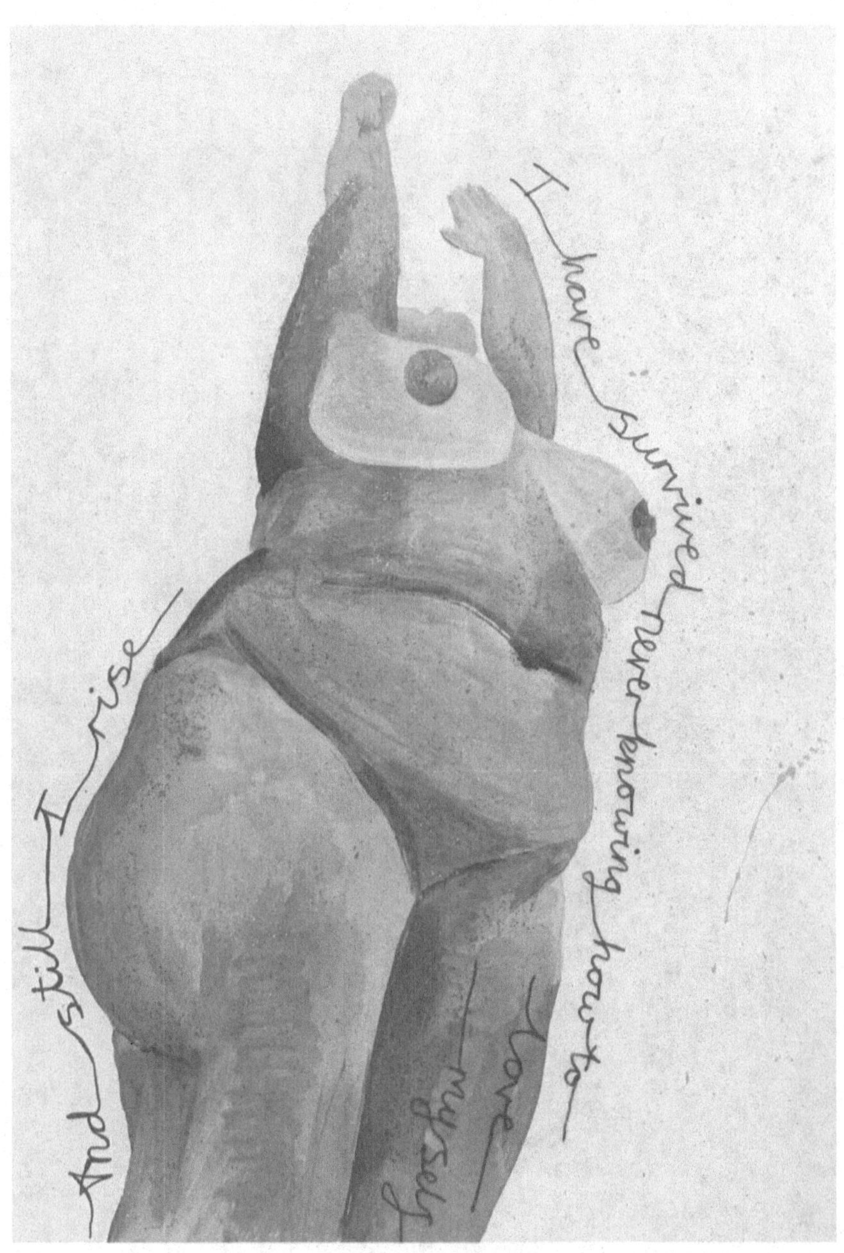

I have survived never knowing how to love myself...
And still, I rise.

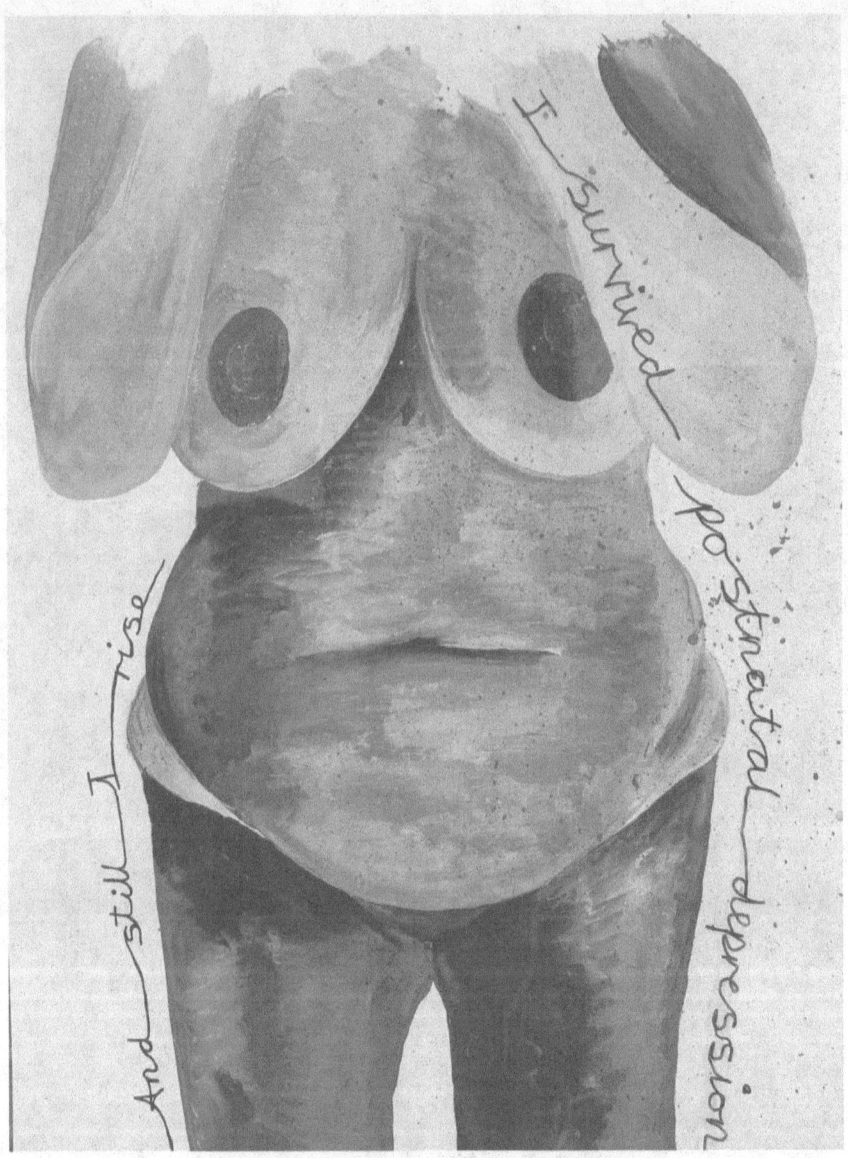

I survived postnatal depression.
I did. But I now love these stretch marks because they are literally
proof of life from my womb that birthed two beautiful sons.

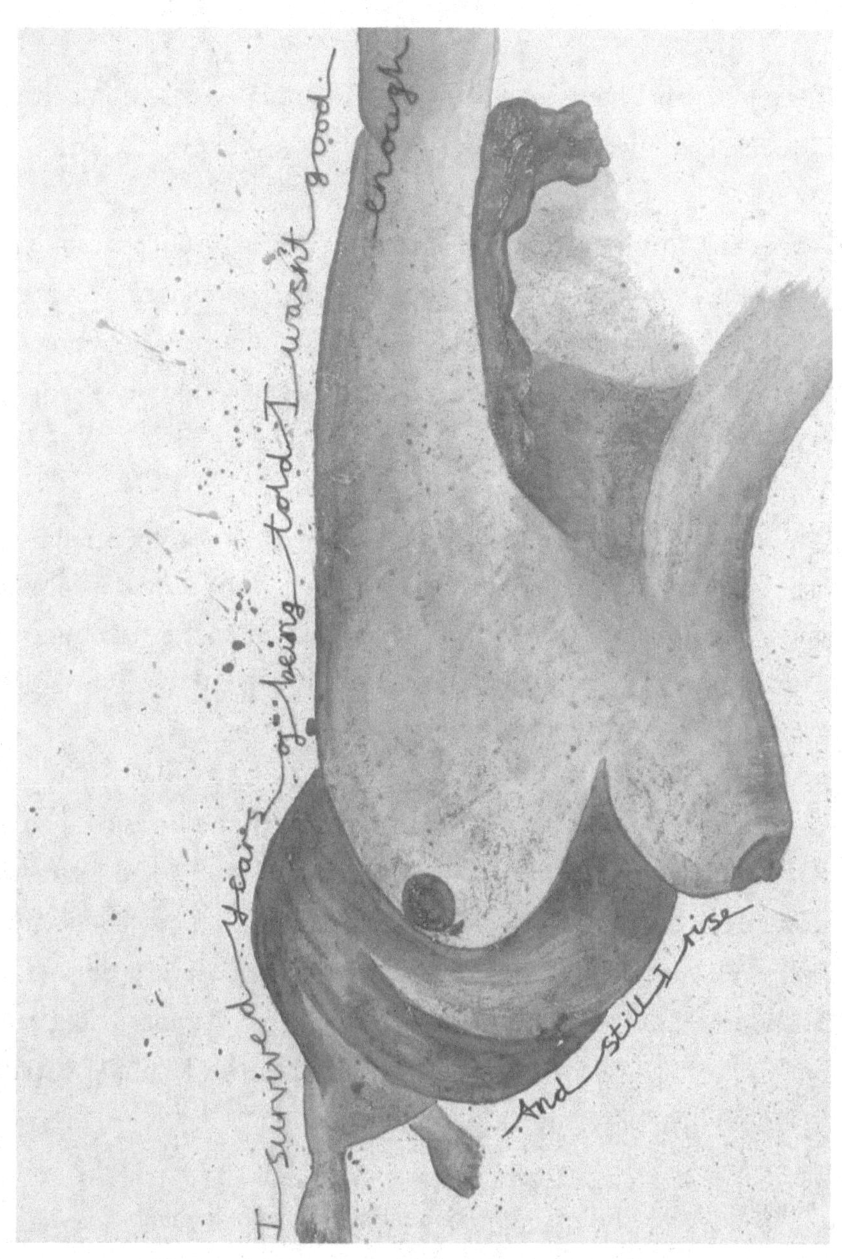

I survived years of being told I wasn't good enough.
And still, I rise.

The Goddess House

Trista Hendren

These last years have taught me to dream big—and embrace the LARGENESS of my heart.

Connecting to the power and love of Goddess through ritual has been a big thing for me lately. The last year, I purchased a Sistrum after being inspired by several of the pieces in our Isis anthology. I have rattled many dreams into existence—and found my strength again.

A few months before that, I purchased an Incantation Bowl, inspired by the words and imagery in Sue Monk Kidd's inspiring novel, *The Book of Longings. In it,* the main character pronounces over her bowl: "Bless the largeness inside me, no matter how I fear it."[27]

For too long, women have played small. It is not surprising, given that for centuries, women were tortured and even killed for their power. For too long, the work of women has been devalued. And that goes beyond the work of mothering and care-taking. Our artistic accomplishments are also undervalued and underpaid. Even feminist work has not been valued—despite the fact that it has done so much for women around the world.

But I feel a real turning point, especially in the last year.

---

[27] Kidd, Sue Monk. *The Book of Longings.* Viking; 2020.

We are collectively reclaiming all the broken and stolen pieces of ourselves.

So, I want to announce my big, big intention—and plan for a Goddess House here in Bergen, where I now live. To stake our claim on this big dream, my husband Anders has begun to reconstruct the giant Willendorf statue pictured here in the anthology with both Tamara and Anique—in our front yard. We have been delayed by a very frozen January and many other obstacles, but remain undeterred.

This statue will not go unnoticed. We want to reignite a movement to put women back front and center—as the living Goddesses that we are.

We toured the museums of Vienna extensively when we visited Tamara and her family. My daughter ate it all up. But I could not help but notice the utter lack of female artists. As the Guerrilla Girls asked on one of their posters, "Do women have to be naked to get into the Met Museum? – Less than 5% of the artists in the Modern Art sections are women, but 85% of the nudes are female."

We plan to have a museum filled with women's art from around the world; artist-in-residence suites; rooms to create all sorts of art; a restaurant and cafe; a library; a gift shop filled with Goddess books, art, jewelry, music and more; a concert hall for Goddess music—and much, much more. We hope to attract visitors from around the world—and school children from throughout the country.

And of course, we will have a Willendorf Room, dedicated to Her!

More importantly, it is my dream to raise enough money for the opening to invite as many of the Foremothers of the Goddess Spirituality movement here as possible—all expenses paid.

So many of these women have given their entire life in service—without much back from all of us. This is not the Goddess way. And it is my intention for all of us doing this work—that we live abundant and glorious lives. And that those benefiting from this work better support the women who have brought forth so much ancient wisdom.

If you would like to help make this dream a reality, make sure to sign up for my mailing list on my website so you can get updates on this project: www.thegirlgod.com.

Finished statue July 29th 2022.

We Are All Venus

Kitty Star

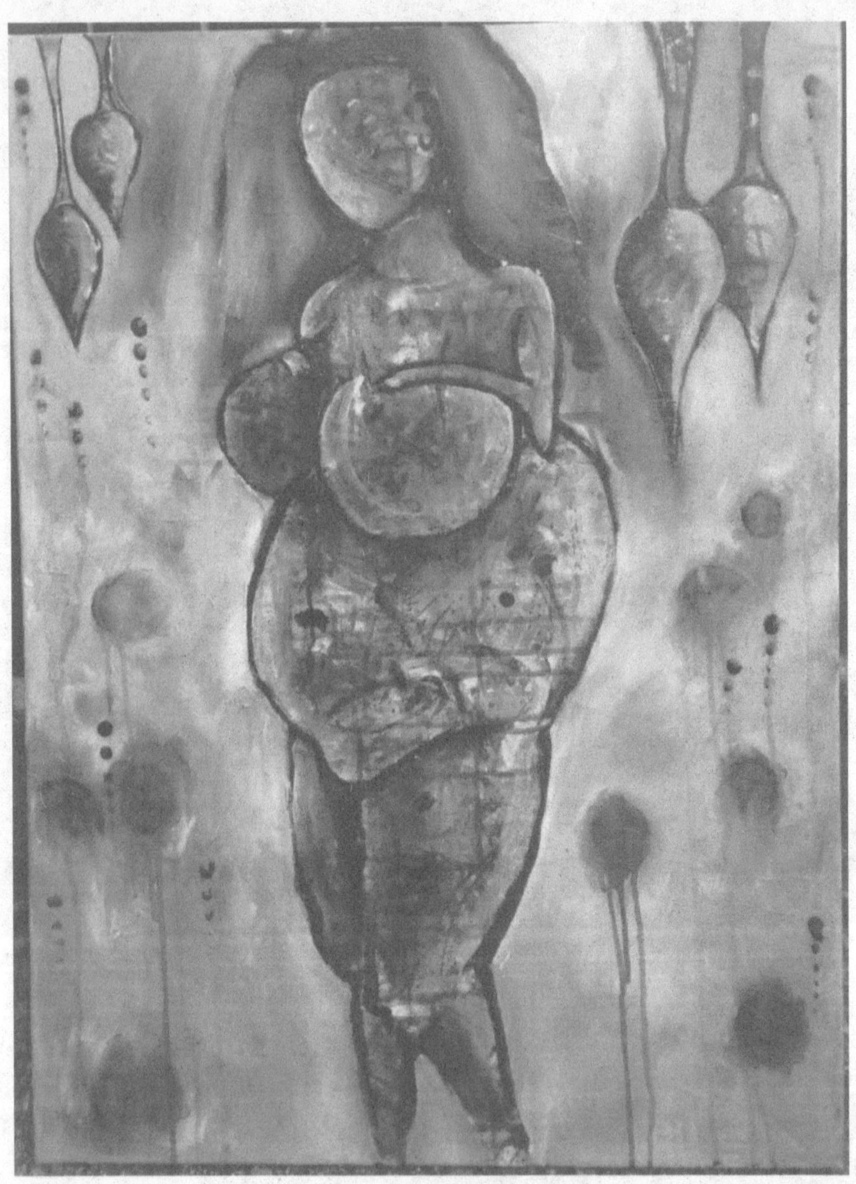

Willendorf: A Decree

Nicola O'Hanlon

And so she woke up from her deep slumber,
disturbed by men who discussed the
reason she came to be,
named her with their insufficiency
and damaged minds,
claimed they knew her
as a tool for their own pleasure.
They were sure they knew.
And in their ignorance
she cast them aside.

And so she woke up,
her body swelled with ancient knowledge
born from a million queens,
she surveyed her land
proud and full,
ready to rule and win
and put the disquiet to rest.
The wind carried to her the
cries of her women.
The taste of their shame tainted what once was
sweet sanctity for the Female,
where men knew nurturing and love.

And so she woke up
But what is this?

"You woman, help your sister up
and hold her higher than yourself.
What has happened to your sacred bodies,
to your blissful hearts?
Why do you make yourself small.
Starving.
Let no man tell you about the
shape of you.
Let no god rip the sacred from you
and render you dead!"

"Wake up Women!
For I am Goddess and I say
you are the most sacred of all!
My women wake up!
Wild and wild and wild
and free
boil your herbs and
read your tarot
and cast your spells
and dance your dreams."

"Wake up Women
Wake up!
For I am Goddess and I say you will."

To Willendorf, With Love
Jen Cooper

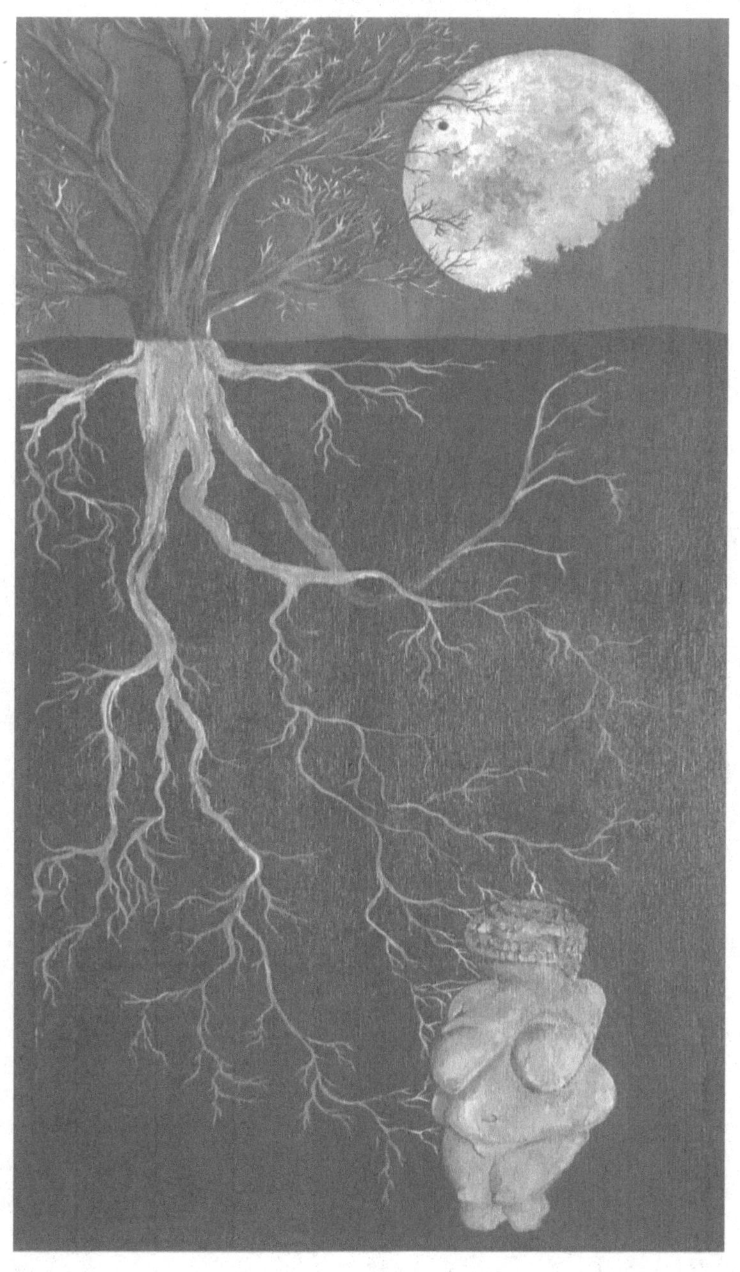

My Body is a Goddess
The Goddess is my Body

Arlene Bailey

My Body is a Goddess
The Goddess is my Body

We are one and the same—
inseparable—
for we are made of the same
stars and planets and
wet moist earth

My Body is Her Body
Her Body is My Body

We have lived lifetimes
enshrined on cave walls,
in temple art and as
hand-carved statues

We are sumptuous and
we are lithe and we
have been worshipped

Her. You. Me. Us.

AND

We have been enslaved as
chattel and possessions,
hunted and killed,
destroyed as evil personified
and evil in stone
We have been told we are
too fat, too thin
too pretty, too ugly
too rich, too poor
too this or too that

We are never just right

And...

Still we exist!

Our Body as Goddess
Goddess as our Body

One and the same
in all shapes and colors
in all sizes and appearances

And we proclaim...

IT. IS. ALL. FUCKING. GOOD!

All bodies are beautiful!

All bodies are desirable!

All bodies are juicy
manifestations of

She Who is BOTH
Goddess and Woman

She who is BOTH
Woman and Goddess

We are perfect in all
our shapes and forms

AND

WE. ARE. RISING!

Untethered to
to societal norms
AND
Unabashedly proud of
WHO we are
and
HOW we are!

For Goddess comes in
all shapes, all colors, all ages
all religions, all nationalities

AND

AS SHE IS
SO ARE WE

ALL birthed from that First Mother
down through the Mother Line,
we are all beautiful
we are all sacred
we are all unique
we are all one

My Body is a Goddess
The Goddess is my Body

My Body is a Goddess, The Goddess is my Body by Arlene Bailey, ©2020

The Flowering
Jassy Watson

A Letter to You from Venus of Willendorf
Words and art by Kat Shaw

Do not hide away. Cover up. Dim your shine.

Do not forget to love yourself. Shrink behind the views of others.

Do not lose yourself. Forget your purpose. Live your life confined within society's perceptions.

Do not do yourself the injustice of belittling yourself. Hating your body. Not honouring your radiance.

Do not conform. Conceal yourself. Hide.

Do not forget how truly magnificent you are in a world where airbrushing is considered normal in order to achieve beauty.

Wake up. Break free. Look at me and walk in my footsteps.

Devour my abundant flesh as you turn your attention to your own.

Love your body—have gratitude for your plentiful, copious, lavish contours.

Kiss your voluptuous rolls and sprinkle adoration onto your wonderous breasts.

Rejoice as your thighs dance to the story of your life. Reconnect with plentiful, divine self-love.

The time is now. Stand together with me.

Honour other women. We are one. One Divine Feminine.
One Goddess. I, we, She. No difference. No separation.

No filters. No shame.

Just perfection, liberation, beauty. Potential, freedom, glory.
Divinity.

Stand in your brilliance and wonder. Rejoice in your perfection.

The power you hold within your curves is waiting to be unlocked.

You are sovereign. Breathe yourself in. I am proud of you.

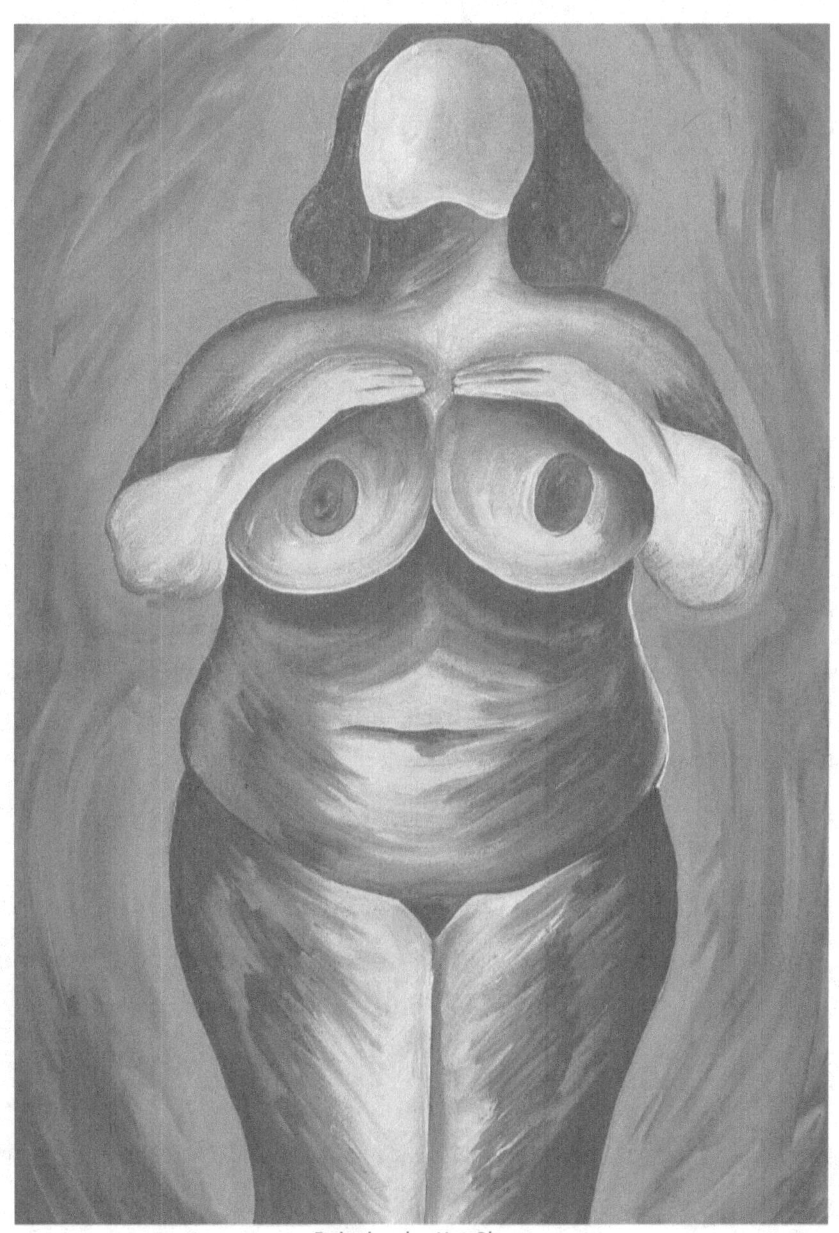

Painting by Kat Shaw

The Gaze of Love:
A Body-Loving Invitation to all Women
Patricia Lynn Reilly

On the way home from a Women's Mindfulness Group, I was filled with gratitude because I had found what I was looking for—an experience of unconditionally loving attention. Out in the world, the attention is judgmental in one way or another. Either the gaze of others finds me attractive and thus worthy of attention, or unattractive and unworthy. I was not alone—women in the circle had experienced the constant assault of body-focused gazes and critiques.

Sarah, a grandmother in the group, felt like Mother Bear whenever she was with her adolescent granddaughter in public places like parks and malls. She felt compelled to shield her granddaughter from the objectifying gazes of men. Sarah was committed to finding ways to fortify her granddaughter's self-esteem and body-acceptance.

In the circle, we acknowledged how painful it was to experience the critical gaze of other women and to recognize that the same inclination was within us. Competitive comparisons had become a daily experience as we looked (or tried to manage the impulse to look) and then sized each other up from head to toe to determine who was thinner and more attractive, who looked younger, and who posed no threat in our competition for attention.

Jenny, a young mother in the group, confessed that she picked her friends from the pool of women she considered less attractive than herself. She instantly sized up women—when she felt out of their league, she became intimidated, hostile, and jealous, and when she felt superior, she pursued friendship. Jenny expressed the need to quiet her inner critical voice so that her relationships would be less manipulative.

We acknowledged our inclination to hide our bodies beneath layers of clothing, our sensuality beneath layers of shame, and our feelings beneath layers of restraint. And most fundamentally, we were all exhausted from hiding the reality of our lives beneath layers of seething resentment in response to and avoidance of the persistent body and weight scrutiny of media images and advertising expectations, of our families, friends, and lovers, and of our own inner critic.

At the final group meeting, Liz read from her journal: "I am shedding my sense of shame about being a woman—and learning to accept my female body. As I heal, I am able to look at myself in the mirror. I am taking dance lessons and receiving massage. I am embracing my body's inevitable aging with compassion and gratitude. Negative feelings come up with these self-caring actions—healing will take time."

Sitting in that group, I felt at peace. Yes, we all wrestled with the same self-critical and competitive demons, but at least the intention of that particular support group was the creation of a safe place for 3 hours a week. In that vulnerable and tender circle, we told the truth, and looked upon each other with mercy, listened to each other with respect, and celebrated life with laughter and solidarity.

My experience in the Mindfulness Group birthed a personal affirmation and a body-loving invitation to the community of women. These expressions emerged in one of those moments when the inner voice grows so loud that you have no other option but to listen to it. I imagine them as gifts from the Mother of All Living, expressing her deep concern for her daughters. I imagine them passing from woman to woman, from mother to daughter in that powerful flow of woman-connection and power.

An Affirmation: "There is No Blemish"

I return to the Breath of Life and I am soothed into acceptance of this moment, just as it is. I am comforted by the truth that I am whole, perfect, and complete in body, mind, and spirit. I rest in acceptance, and all is well.

There is no blemish in me. I am the Daughter of Life and my body is lovely just as it is, in its perfect shape and size. I am at peace—the war is over. There is only comfort, soothing, and acceptance.

I am at home in my body. I am at ease with my body's sensations. I am at play with my body's sensuality and at peace with my body's natural cycles. I speak about my body with reverence. And so it is.

An Invitation: "The Gaze of Love"

Today, and every day, may we turn toward our own bodies and the bodies of all women with mercy and unconditional acceptance. May we let go of the competitive, scrutiny-based sizing up of each other and the put-downs and diminishments expressed when we're threatened by each other. May we allow healing attention to flow one to another until the gaze of love heals us all.

A gaze of love, calling wise women with their beautiful silver hair and life-lines out of hiding. A gaze of love, inviting our smart and gifted daughters to reject the tyranny of thinness and to cease from harming themselves.

A gaze of love, welcoming the full, rounded bodies of our friends, bodies that refuse to be battered into shape by diets and admonishments.

A gaze of love so powerful and encompassing, that it embraces the entire community of women, all sizes, shapes, colors, ages, and languages, with the widest welcome, the deepest affirmation, the highest calling, and the strongest YES.

A gaze of love, inspiring us to bite into life and the fullness of its possibility; to express life through us in color and shape, sound and movement; and to honor life by turning our body-loving energy toward projects of justice, relationships of comfort, strategies of wellness, and words of affirmation.

We are all in this together. One breath. One body. One life. And so it is.

An excerpt from *Love Your Body Regardless: From Body-Judgment to Body-Acceptance*.

I Am God

Alyscia Cunningham

The Body as Deity

Trista Hendren

"This is the core of our task: to respect and revere ourselves, and so bring about a world in which women are respected and revered, recognized once again as holding the life-giving power of the earth itself." -Sharon Blackie[28]

Over the last decade, I have tried to put as many women's words out into books and social media as possible. I feel it is critically important to hear quotes by women and in particular, women's stories. *We have wasted so much of our lives absorbed in the narratives of men.*

Increasingly, I am realizing that we also need to come back into our bodies and reclaim them before the words can fully sink in.

When I was trying to cope with the relapse of my ex-husband and our subsequent divorce, I began to read a lot. But in retrospect, it was Kundalini Yoga that saved my life and my sanity. No amount of knowledge could cause me to take the actions I needed to. I had to reconnect with my body and my soul—both of which had been severely abused.

I was fortunate to grow up with a full-figured mother who never criticized my weight. I feel a relative acceptance with this body of mine, which is one of the greatest gifts my mother gave me.

---

[28] Blackie, Sharon. *If Women Rose Rooted: A Life-changing Journey to Authenticity and Belonging.* September Publishing; 2019.

On the other hand, I grew up with a stepfather who could best be described as *unkind*—to all of us, in different ways. He treated my mom's weight with contempt, making jokes at her expense in front of other people.

I was a late bloomer. I did not start my menses until I was nearly 16—probably because I was very thin. I went from an A cup to a D cup in 6 months during my 17th year—and began sprouting elsewhere too. I remember my stepfather poking me in the belly one day, telling me I had better *watch it*. It never occurred to him that he had better watch *himself* and stop coming into my bedroom to molest me.

It has taken me decades to reclaim my body as my own—although I regrettably am not all the way there yet. Most recently, dream work has been the most effective means of healing from my trauma—particularly the parts I was not ready to confront in my earlier years.

What I have realized these last years is that I became disconnected from this body of mine at some point during my childhood. It's like my body doesn't really belong to *me*.

Many of us have been taught this (to some extent) from the get-go due to forced hugs or childhood sexual abuse—or the rapes or threat of rape that many of us endure over the course of our lifetimes.

In my haze of raising children, keeping up a house, working, volunteering and everything else the modern mother does—I continue to 'live' on autopilot. Like many mothers, I shovel in food without tasting it. I never "have time" to do my beloved Kundalini Yoga or Qi Gong. There is always someone else's need (or want) that is more pressing—more important.

About a decade ago, I composed a vow of faithfulness to myself using Patricia Lynn Reilly's *I Promise Myself* book. It's an amazing and life-affirming process that I recommend to all women. However, like any relationship, you must continue to honor and re-affirm your vows, or they will break down.

The vows that are always hardest for me to keep involve honoring my own body. This is heartbreaking to recognize because it is this body that houses my soul—and, I believe, the spirit of Goddess that resides in each of us.

I have always loved Sonya Renee Taylor's poem which inspired her movement: *The Body is not an Apology.*

> "Praise for the body, for the body is not an apology. The body is deity. The body is God, the body is God."[29]

To hear her recite the entire poem is a healing experience in and of itself.

And yet, most of us are completely disconnected from our divinity. In fact, women have so much body hatred that plastic surgery and other body 'fixes' have become a multi-billion-dollar industry. Dr. Gail Dines is quoted as saying, "If tomorrow, women woke up and

---

[29] Taylor, Sonya Renee. *"The Body is not an Apology."* July 2010. ©Sonya Renee Taylor.

decided they really liked their bodies, just think how many industries would go out of business."

Like many women, pregnancy and birth were when the gig was up for me. As a young, unmarried professional who had not planned to get pregnant quite yet, I hid my first pregnancy under my suit jackets for the first 7 months. I worked my regular 50+ hour workweek until the night I gave birth. But something clicked when I went into labor. I felt so much POWER giving birth to my son.

I did not try to hide my AWESOMELY HUGE belly or work insane hours while pregnant with my daughter. After a lifetime of living under patriarchy—this was the first time that I felt in my body my POWER as a woman and as a CREATOR.

I finally named and claimed my hunger—and devoured several large meals one after another from my favorite Italian restaurant after each birth. In fact, I ate whatever the fuck I wanted throughout each pregnancy and years of breastfeeding that followed. It seems insane now to realize that this was entirely *new* to me. It was the first time in my life that I did not agonize over each bite of food. It was the first time in my life that I felt like I had the *right* to eat.

So, while I know that the Willendorf is more likely a Grandmother archetype, Alyscia Cunningham's *I Am God* photo series resonates deeply for me when I think of proclaiming our divinity as women. I am reminded of a quote by Mary Daly:

> "There is nothing like the sound of women really laughing!
> The roaring laughter of women is like the roaring of the
> eternal sea. Hags can cackle and roar at themselves, but

more and more, one hears them roaring at the reversal that is patriarchy, that monstrous jock's joke, the Male Mothers Club that gives birth only to putrefaction and deception... But this laughter is the one true hope, for as long as it is audible, there is evidence that someone is seeing through the Dirty Joke."[30]

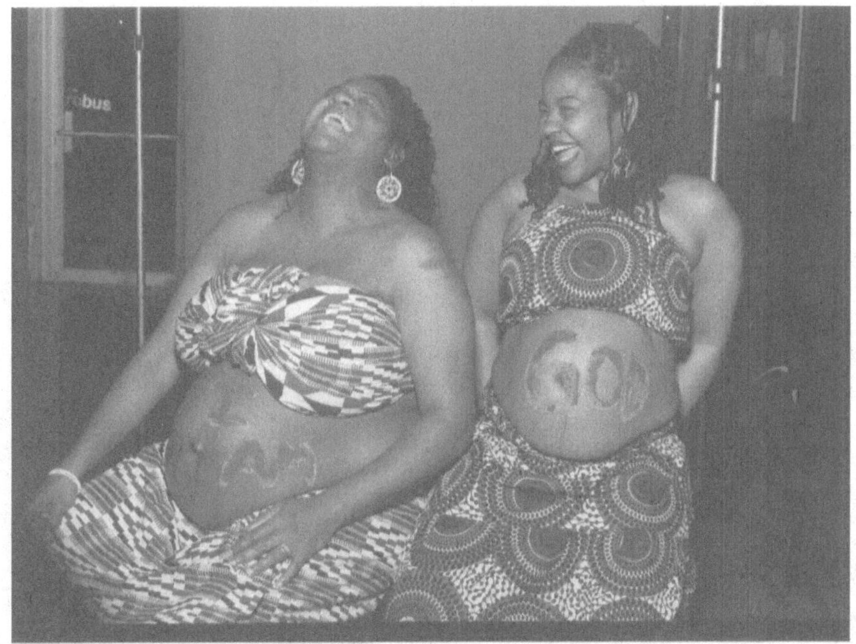

Photo by Alyscia Cunningham

A dirty joke is exactly what all of this is. All the self-hatred, body-shaming and everything else robs women of our vital life-energy and divinity.

We must begin to reclaim a world for all of us where our bodies are holy, adored and treasured.

---

[30] Daly, Mary. *Gyn/Ecology: The Metaethics of Radical Feminism.* Beacon Press; 1990.

I am not certain that we can affirm ourselves into loving our bodies, although it can help. I believe we need to take action—whether it be dancing naked with other women—or taking a self-defense class, doing Yoga at home or savoring a meal. We have to stop telling ourselves to love our bodies and actually live our lives in a way that *is* love. We must love and worship our bodies as if they were the Goddess Herself.

So, here is an affirmation I try to remember daily:

> *Your body is Goddess in one of Her most beautiful forms.*
> *Love Her fiercely.*

May it be so—for all of us.

Coloring Sheet

Arna Baartz

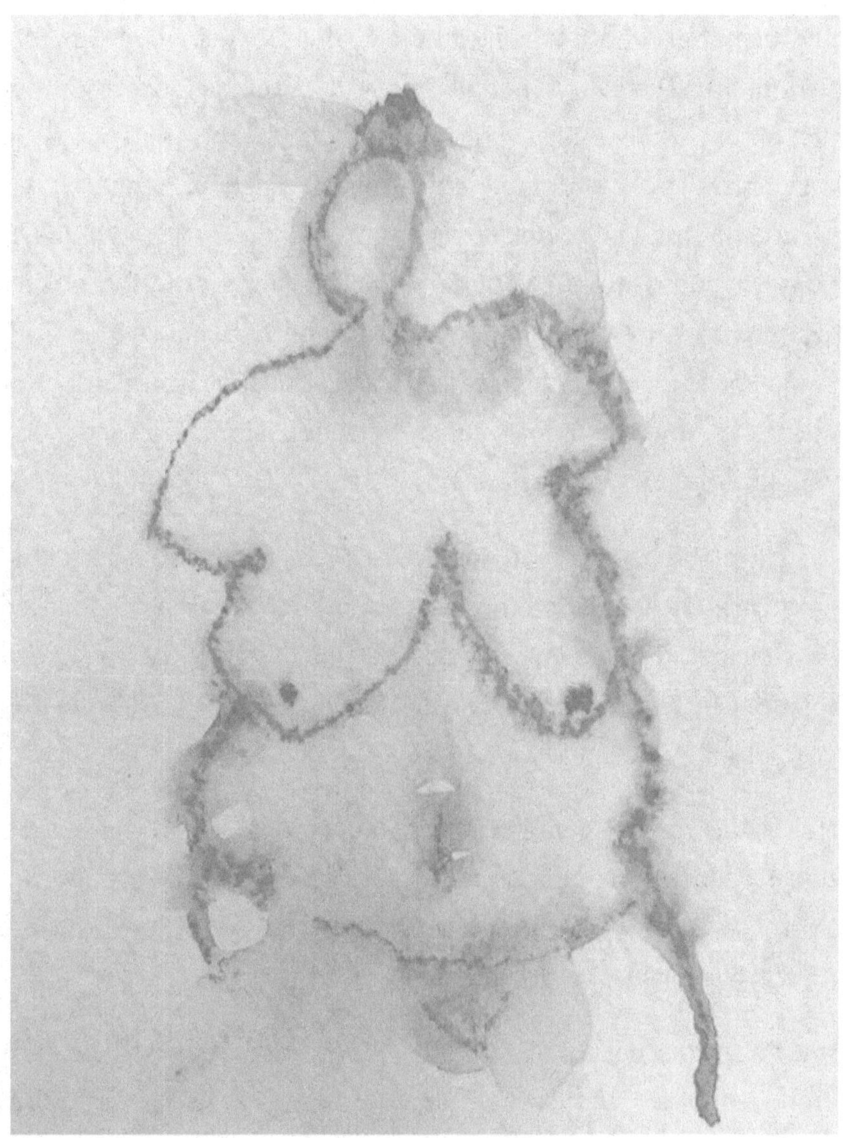

Illustration from My Name is Goddess of Willendorf by Tamara Albanna

List of Contributors

Alyscia Cunningham is an entrepreneur, author, filmmaker, and photographer who has contributed to the *Smithsonian, National Geographic, Discovery Channel* and *AOL*. After the success of her first book, *Feminine Transitions*, a photography book encompassed with portraits of raw feminine beauty, Cunningham published her second photography book documentary film, *I Am More Than My Hair*. It includes interviews and of females who've experienced hair loss due to a health-related condition and their journey of self-empowerment to see beauty beyond the media's standards. Her upcoming documentary, *Seeing*, includes stories of girls and woman who are visually impaired.

Alyscia is the Founder of *Her House Media* and also one of the FrontLine Voices for *Stop the Beauty Madness*, a campaign focused on changing the dynamics of beauty globally. Her work has been featured in *The Huffington Post, Cosmopolitan, The Washington Post, Fox 5, ABC 7* and *Proud2BMe*.

Her goal is to continuing producing documentary films and photo books. With the completion and direction provided through the Horror/Psychological Thriller workshop with Sundance Institute, Alyscia also plans to write and direct Horror films.

Alyscia invites you to view her video introductions to *Feminine Transitions* and *I Am More Than My Hair*. To learn more about Alyscia and her work, visit Alyscia.com.

Anique Radiant Heart is High Priestess of the Global Goddess, Goddess Scholar, Sacred Singer Songwriter, author of *Chanting the Chakras – A Way to the Goddess Through Energetic Use of Voice* and *The 33 Teachings of Kuan Yin* and an internationally acclaimed Spiritual Teacher. Anique Radiant Heart is a well-loved member of the International Goddess Community.

A wise crone now at 73—for the past 43 years, Anique has created CDs of original music celebrating the Goddess, produced Goddess festivals, conferences, and led tours to sacred sites all over the world. In 2007, she was crowned a Foremother of the Australian Goddess Community at the Australian Goddess Conference. In 2010, she manifested the Temple of the Global Goddess for all to enjoy, and began teaching a 3-year Priestess Training program in the Temple of the Global Goddess in Maitland. Today, there are 2 Temples of the Global Goddess – the Mother House in Maitland and the Sister House in Sydney. She now has a dedicated grove of ordained Priestesses with another round of training which began in 2017. Anique has organized Goddess Conferences and Festivals in Australia since 1996, and for the past 4 years has been the co-visionary with respected Aboriginal Elder Bilawara Lee of the Australian Goddess Conference – the first Conference ever in Australia to be held by an Aboriginal and Non-Aboriginal sister.

In 2017, at the Glastonbury Goddess Conference, Anique revealed and launched her Vision for an International Priestess Convocation, to take place in Crete in 2020. This gathering is designed to put into place strategies to bring about the unfolding of The Motherworld – a platform for social, political and spiritual change in the world.

Dedicated to assisting women to reclaim their natural spiritual authority, Anique continues to teach women the power and joy that comes from a sacred path which celebrates the Divine Feminine. For the last 25 years, she has travelled for 3 months each year to share her teachings and music with daughters and sons of the Goddess all over the world.

http://goddess.net.au/

Annie Caplan is a fine art film photographer focused on helping women build confidence and see their true beauty through intimate portraiture during all stages of life. Her sessions are about honoring your body and story while cheering you on in your journey to self-love. As a certified nutritional therapist, she also creates content for authentic and heart-driven wellness brands. Annie believes in a holistic approach to health where both the mind and body are lovingly nurtured.

Kohenet Annie Matan is a Jewish, feminist, queer, Hebrew Priestess and Mama. She facilitates sacred community, weaves transformative ritual and empowers intuitives, mystics and healers to own and share their gifts for the sake of the interindependent healing and transformation of the world.

Arlene Bailey is a visionary artist and author working in the realm of the Sacred Female in all her many visages. Arlene's paintings and poetry/prose reflect the raw, visceral and sacred wild in all women, while challenging and questioning everything we know to be true about *the who* of who we are as women walking in this time.

Through her magical weavings in word and paint—and, drawing on her trainings and skills as an Ordained Priestess, Women's

Mysteries Facilitator, Wise Woman Herbalist, Energy Medicine Practitioner and Retired Anthropologist—Arlene invites women to step into personal sovereignty as they listen to their ancient memories and voice of their soul.

Published in several Girl God Books' anthologies, Arlene is also a monthly contributor to *Return to Mago* E-Magazine and has writings in two forthcoming Mago anthologies. Her work can also be found on *The Sacred Wild*, a page on Facebook about re-wilding woman's soul.

Along with her partner and five cats, this Wild Crone lives on 18 acres of deep woods and quartz outcroppings in the Uwharrie Mountains of North Carolina, USA.

www.facebook.com/sacredwildstudio
www.instagram.com/arlenebaileyartist
www.magobooks.com
www.magoism.net

Arna Baartz is a painter, writer/poet, martial artist, educator and mother to eight fantastic children. She has been expressing herself creatively for more than 50 years and finds it to be her favourite way of exploring her inner being enough to evolve positively in an externally-focused world. Arna's artistic and literary expression is her creative perspective of the stories she observes playing out around her. Claims to fame: Arna has been selected for major art prizes and won a number of awards, published many books, and— (her favourite) was being used as a 'paintbrush' at the age of two by well-known Australian artist John Olsen. Arna lives and works from her bush studio in the Northern Rivers, NSW Australia. Her website is www.artofkundalini.com

Brenda Oelbaum is a conceptual, multi-disciplinary, social practice artist whose work is deeply rooted in the tenets of feminism. Over the years her work has become increasingly performative and community driven. Inspired by pop culture and current events, she finds humor in the odd juxtapositions that inform her art making. After 10 years of service to the board of National Women's Caucus for Art; she is once again back the studio, looking forward to the culmination of her Venus of Willendorf Project. In February 2013, Oelbaum installed her first diet book maze at Whitdel Arts, Detroit, as a test run, of her proposed "Diet World." This ongoing project is a physical and visual attack, or commentary on the US government's so called "War on Obesity" and the multi-billion dollar diet industry.

Oelbaum holds a BFA equivalent from the Ontario College of Art in Toronto, Canada; where she studied painting in Florence, Italy under the direction of the late Aba Bayefski and received an MA in Gallery Administration from F.I.T. in New York. She has worked with such prominent art dealers as Rosa Esman, and Gracie Mansion in NYC. Currently Oelbaum is the representative for the Feminist Art Project. She is an avid collector of art, and feels one of the best ways to support women in the arts is to collect their work.

Though **Daniel Cox** is a professionally trained paqo (shaman) of the Inca tradition, he is now implementing traditional British witchcraft into his spiritual practise. As a follower of the Goddess faith, Daniel has dedicated his life's work to not only healing the wounded feminine within women and men, but to bring her alive in his art and his writing. Daniel lives on the edge of an English wood with his husband and their son.

Sparked by an initiation as a Red Tent Priestess, **Elizabeth Ogletree** set out to solidify a thriving red tent community for the women of Denver, CO, gathering every month on the New Moon since October 2015. Inspired to follow this path by her Grandmother Sue, a woman who wore red every day of her life and who died when Elizabeth was 9 of ovarian cancer, Elizabeth felt a deeper need for women to rediscover ancient ways of maintaining womb health through ritual and magick. Through her dynamic and spiritually rich visions and paintings of the Goddess and her unique approach to working with the magick of the menstrual cycle in ceremony, Elizabeth provides inspiration, creative encouragement, and space holding for women in her circles, offerings, and artwork. www.moonandwomb.com

Fig Ally lives in northern New Mexico between Santa Fe and Los Alamos. A second volume of her poetry, *Measures of Wonder 2* will be out March 2021 as companion to her previously published first volume, *Measures of Wonder*. Her short writing has also been featured in several publications including *Autobiographies of Our Orgasms*. Her short play, *The Daughters of Elvis* christened the opening of the Logan O'Neil Theatre in Chicago and toured nationwide for a year. September, 2021 will see Fig in a collaborative short film featuring women poets on the pandemic in our hearts. Fig is also a world drummer in the international Womens Drumsong Orchestra.

Glen Rogers is an internationally exhibited artist—painter, printmaker and sculptor—from the United States who has lived in Mexico for the last 20 years. She currently splits her time between Mazatlán and San Miguel de Allende, MX. She has created more than 25 public artworks including: *Beacon*, Campbell, CA; *Three Wings*, Stockton, CA; *Web of Life*, Chico, CA; *Spirit Gate* and *Meditation Bench*, San Jose, CA. She has published two books—*Art and Sacred Sites: Connecting with Spirit of Place* and *Symbols of the Spirit: A Meditative Journey Through Art*—and her most recent, *Spirit Cards*, a deck of 50 oracle cards.

Visit her website to see what else she's up to:
www.glenrogersart.com
Read her blog for the backstory:
www.artandsacredsites.com
glen@glenrogersart.com

Hollie Holden is a mother, artist, writer and ordained Interfaith Spirit minister with One Spirit. She teaches parenting, spirituality and Enneagram workshops in person and shares her wisdom online with her Facebook community, Notes on Living & Loving https://www.facebook.com/hollieholdenlove.
Her website is: http://www.hollieholden.me/

Jakki Moore is an Irish artist, storyteller and cartoonist. She is particularly fond of projects concerning human and animal rights. She is currently working on a book about animals.

Jassy Watson is a contemporary Australian artist living on the glorious sub-tropical Queensland coast. You will find her working full-time from her garden studio and beachside gallery set among the sugar cane fields, red dirt and coral coastline of the Bundaberg region. While formally trained in the arts in her early years, a life of experimenting and exploring led Jassy to develop a unique way of working with images that feel genuine. She works primarily in acrylics and mixed media but has more recently returned to oils as her preferred medium. Her use of materials is bold and assertive, especially evident in her use of heavy black inky lines, and a palette as vibrant as nature itself.

Jassy's paintings are largely inspired by scenes of the everyday that she records as part of her daily drawing practice. From the lounge to the ever-changing landscape of her region to tropical Bali and even her own backyard, her larger than life paintings are captivating, at times sentimental, while contrastingly quirky in perspective. With an intentional, intuitive and confident approach, Jassy's deep connection to land and place truly shines through in these unique interpretations of the world around her.

Her work hangs in private and public collections and has been selected and exhibited in numerous solo, group and award shows at leading galleries, with her most recent solo *The Sacred and Mundane; Scenes of the Everyday* exhibited by Hervey Bay Regional Art Gallery. Further, her paintings have also been featured in a number of international online and in-text publications, including journals, blogs, university textbooks, published books and other texts. Most recently, her work has appeared in the Summer edition of Australia's National *Art/Edit* magazine. While most of her work is done at the canvas, Jassy is also very passionate about sharing her artistic skill and wisdom with others. As a certified Intentional Creativity® teacher she has been teaching from her home studio and travelling the globe offering educational programs and retreats for the past 8 years.

For more information, go to Jassy.com.au

Jen Cooper is an ecologist, artist, and mother living on the shore of Sydney Harbour, Canada. Blending art and science, she focuses our world through a lens trained on the web between the details. Her artworks are painted on reclaimed wood and held together with screws and wires harvested from expired objects, because science holds wonder but also truth—a piece that diverts waste seems to be more honest. Delighting in anarchy, Cooper transcends pigeon holes by using art to explore biology and archaeology, and imagination to inspire scientific understanding, reaching back for messages from our ancestors on how to live today.

Joey Hartmann-Dow is an artist and activist based in New Orleans, LA. She is the creator of the Badass Women Project and Us & We Art. You can find her work at thebadasswomen.com.

Kat Shaw prides herself on breaking through the stereotypical views of beauty that have been cast upon society by the media, having made her name painting the glorious reality that is a woman's body.

Her nude studies of real women garnered unprecedented popularity within only a few short months, as women were crying out for themselves to be portrayed in art, rather than the airbrushed images of the perfection of the female form that are so rife in today's culture.

After graduating with a fine art degree, Kat achieved a successful full-time teaching career for 14 years, and continues to teach art part-time whilst passionately pursuing her mission of world domination by empowering as many women as possible to reach their fullest potential by embracing their bodies and loving themselves wholeheartedly.

Kat spreads her inspirational magic through her artwork, her Wellbeing business, "Fabulously Imperfect", and her dedication to Goddess energy.

Reiki is a huge part of her life, and as a Reiki Master, Kat is committed to sharing Reiki, teaching Usui, Angelic and Karuna Reiki, and channelling Reiki energy through her artwork to uplift and heal.

As a Sister of Avalon, Kat also works directly with her Goddess consciousness, connecting to Goddess and Priestess energy and translating it into Divine Feminine-infused paintings to inspire women and spread Goddess love.

Kat is also mum to a gorgeous teenage daughter, a bellydancer and an avid pioneer in improving the lives of rescue animals.

Kitty Star is a mother, artist, therapist and freedom fighter living in a yurt in the wilds of Cornwall. She is passionate about helping women to reconnect with their sexual and reproductive anatomy and sexual energy, restoring honour to the female body and restoring humanity's severed connection to Mother Earth.

Leonor Murciano-Luna, PhD, IMD, AP is an author, spiritual healer and teacher, artist, holistic doctor and acupuncture physician.

A Healer & Feminine Guide, she has spent the last 25 years committed to helping women heal their hearts and bodies... by stepping into their true Essence, and reclaiming themselves physically, mentally, emotionally and spiritually. Dr. Murciano is the founder of Conscious Feminine Medicine TM, a non-profit organization, the School of Conscious Feminine Medicine, and Nourishing Women, South Florida clinic. She is known as the Healer of Healers... and a leader in the Feminine movement of the time of Great Awakening.

Dr. Murciano is the mother of three beautiful young women, each thriving in their own unique way. She continues to coach, write, teach, mentor, heal and empower women all around the world. For more information on personal spiritual coaching or mentorship and upcoming events, please visit ConsciousFeminineMedicine.com

Luisah Teish is a storyteller-writer, an artist-activist and spiritual guidance counselor. She is an initiated elder (Iyanifa) in the Ifa/ Orisha tradition of the West African Diaspora.

She is the author of *Jambalaya: The Natural Woman's Book of Personal Charms and Practical Rituals*, and she co-authored *On Holy Ground: Commitment and Devotion to Sacred Land* with Kahuna Leilani Birely. Her most recent work is *Spirit Revealing, Color Healing*, a book of Zen Doodles.

She has contributed to 35 anthologies, notably *Spiritual Guidance Across Religions: A Sourcebook for Spiritual Directors and Other Professionals Providing Counsel...* by Rev. John R. Mabry Ph.D., Dan Mendelsohn Aviv Ph.D., Mans Broo Ph.D. and Rev. Cathleen Cox MAT MDiv (Apr 1, 2014) and magazines such as *Ms., Essence, SageWoman*, and the *Yoga Journal*.

She has articles and artwork in *Coreopsis: Journal of Myth and Theater,* and the *Cascadia Subduction Zone Journal of Speculative Fiction.*

Her performance credits include:
Concert for All Beings, Marin Civic Center (2014);
Resonant Streams: An Ancient Call. St. John the Divine Cathedral, New York (2011);
The Praises for the World Concert, directed by Jennifer Berezan, Edge of Wonder Music. (2005);
She has performed in Europe, Venezuela, New Zealand and the United States.

She teaches online courses, provides editorial assistance, facilitates conferences and weekend workshops, and performs in theaters worldwide.
https://www.yeyeluisahteish.com/
https://ileorunmilaoshun.com/

Lydia Ruyle, also known as Ya-Ya, lived to be an 81-year old crone and matriarch who passed away in March 2016. She was an artist and scholar who had been pursuing Goddess research for decades. Her Goddess Banners depict sacred images of the Divine Feminine from the many cultures of the world. Since 1995, the icons have become spirit banners, which flew around the globe weaving the sacred energies of the Divine Feminine. Her research into sacred images of women took her around the globe. She created and exhibited her art, did workshops and led women's journeys throughout the U.S. and internationally. Lydia was the author of two books. *Goddesses of the Americas* was published in 2016 and *Goddess Icons* was published in 2002.

How did Lydia find the Goddess? She called her and she listened. The Goddess asked her to listen, see, touch, learn, laugh, cry and share with art, stories and sacred places of Mother Earth.

Over 30 years ago, she began collecting images of women from art history, which she taught at the University of Northern Colorado in Greeley, Colorado. In 2010, the university created the Lydia Ruyle Room of Women's Art to continue Lydia's mission to teach. In March 1987, an art exhibition at the Loveland Museum and Gallery in Loveland, Colorado called "Better Homes & Goddesses" was the first display of Goddess icons, born for National Women's History Month. In 1993, Lydia invited other women to travel to sacred places with Goddess tours in England, Wales, and Cornwall. Over 300 women joined her to travel in 14 countries.

Lydia made her first Goddess Banners in the series for an exhibition in 1995 at the Celsus Library in Ephesus, Turkey where they flew and spread their energies throughout the month of July. The banner collection grew from 18 to over 300. She used them to empower, teach, and share their stories at sacred sites in 38 countries.

Max Dashu is a land-walker and history sibyl who uses images to teach women's global history and heritages. Her legendary slideshows bring to light women of power who have been hidden from view, from ancient icons to female leaders, culture-makers, rebels, and medicine women. In 1970 Dashu founded the Suppressed Histories Archives to research women in the global cultural record. From her collection of over 30,000 images, Dashu has created and presented hundreds of slideshows at universities, women's centers, bookstores, conferences, festivals, libraries, prisons, museums, and schools. She has presented at international conferences in Italy, Switzerland, Britain, Australia, Germany, Mexico, Bulgaria, Guatemala, and the US. She also teaches via webcasts, online courses, audio podcasts, her blog Veleda, and via daily Suppressed Histories posts on Facebook. Some of her videos are now available as stream on demand via the Suppressed Histories Portal on Teachable.

Max is the author of *Witches and Pagans: Women in European Folk Religion*, the first volume to be published from her sourcebook *Secret History of the Witches*. Her most recent publication is the *Deasophy Coloring Book*. The next is *Pythias, Melissae and Pharmakides: Women in Hellenic culture*, on women's ceremonial culture as well as the roots of rape culture and colonial domination. Max has produced two dvds: *Woman Shaman: the Ancients* (2013) and *Women's Power in Global Perspective* (2008). She is also an artist whose paintings are well known in the women's spirituality community.

Website: suppressedhistories.net
Facebook: facebook.com/Suppressed-Histories-Archives
YouTube: youtube.com/user/maxdashu

Molly Remer has been gathering the women to circle, sing, celebrate, and share since 2008. She plans and facilitates seasonal retreats and rituals, mother-daughter circles, family ceremonies, and red tent circles in rural Missouri. She is a priestess who holds MSW, M.Div, and D.Min degrees and wrote her dissertation about contemporary priestessing in the US. Molly and her husband Mark co-create Story Goddesses, original Goddess sculptures, ceremony kits, mini Goddesses, and more at Brigid's Grove.

Molly is the author of *Womanrunes, Earthprayer, the Goddess Devotional, Whole and Holy, She Lives Her Poems, Sunlight on Cedar, Whole and Holy, She Lives Her Poems, Walking with Persephone* (forthcoming from Womancraft Publishing) and *The Red Tent Resource Kit.* She writes about thealogy, nature, practical priestessing, and the Goddess at *Patreon, Brigid's Grove, Feminism and Religion*, and *Sage Woman* Magazine.

You can find her glorious creations on brigidsgrove.etsy.com and patreon.com/brigidsgrove

Nicola O'Hanlon is an Irish writer of essays and poetry on Feminism, Civil Rights, Mental Health and Addiction. She has a background in Holistic Health practices and care of the elderly. She lives with her partner, two children and an array of cats and dogs on the southeast coast of Ireland in a farmhouse behind tall trees.

Pat Daly (editor) is a mother of three daughters and proud grandma. A published author / writer on career and job search issues, Pat lives in Portland, Oregon. She has tirelessly edited everything that Girl God Books has published—more than 26 books to-date!

Patricia Lynn Reilly has been inspiring women for over 25 years. Her iconic books, poems, and trainings have traveled around the world. Patricia's earlier books include: *A God Who Looks Like Me: Discovering a Woman-Affirming Spirituality, Be Full of Yourself: The Journey from Self-Criticism to Self-Celebration, Imagine a Woman in Love with Herself: Embracing Your Wholeness & Wisdom, I Promise Myself: Making a Commitment to Yourself & Your Dreams* and *Words Made Flesh: An Anthology of Poetry and Prose.*

Pegi Eyers is the author of the award-winning book *Ancient Spirit Rising: Reclaiming Your Roots & Restoring Earth Community*, a survey on social justice, decolonization, nature spirituality, earth-emergent healing and the holistic principles of sustainable living. Pegi self-identifies as a Celtic Animist, and is an advocate for the recovery of authentic ancestral wisdom and traditions for all people. She lives in the countryside on the outskirts of Nogojiwanong in Michi Saagiig Nishnaabeg territory (Ontario, Canada), on a hilltop with views reaching for miles in all directions. www.stonecirclepress.com

Philomena van Rijswijk is a Tasmanian poet, novelist and story-writer. Her magic realist novel, *The World as a Clockface* was published by Penguin in 2001, and follows a woman's journey around the four quarters of the globe. Her dystopian novel, *House of the Flight Helpers,* published by Tartarus Press UK in 2019, focuses on borders, institutionalisation of the marginalised and xenophobia. She also paints in a naive style informed by both the sacred and more mundane feminine. Her inspiration is Granma Moses who said: "If I hadn't painted, I would have kept chickens." She is currently exploring her Prussian heritage, and its associated folklore, especially the complex meanings inherent in the figure of Baba Yaga.

Sharon Smith is a writer, ghost writer, editor, and proofreader with a passion for helping women reconnect with their Authentic Selves and Voices. She loves and honors the Great Mother in all Her many forms, and has a deep connection to Nature. She identifies as a Green Witch and follows an eclectic spiritual path that is a blending of Native American and Celtic Teachings, both in her ancestral line.

Tamara Albanna has always been connected to the Goddess, even when she didn't realize it. As a Doula and Childbirth Educator, she witnessed divinity first-hand through other women. Now as a writer, Reiki healer and Tarot reader, she hopes to help others overcome their difficult pasts while healing with the Divine Mother. She has published two books on Inanna—*Inanna's Ascent: Reclaiming Female Power* (co-edited with Trista Hendren and Pat Daly) and *My Name is Inanna*—as well as two poetry chapbooks, *As I Lay By the Tigris and Weep, Rosewater* and *Kismet*. Her most recent children's book is *My Name is Goddess of Willendorf*. Tamara currently resides in Vienna with her family.

Trista Hendren founded Girl God Books in 2011 to support a necessary unraveling of the patriarchal world view of divinity. Her first book—*The Girl God*, a children's picture book—was a response to her own daughter's inability to see herself reflected in God. Since then, she has published more than 50 books by a dozen women from across the globe with help from her family and friends. Originally from Portland, Oregon, she lives in Bergen, Norway. You can learn more about her projects at www.thegirlgod.com.

Acknowledgments

I would like to acknowledge my co-editors. My mother, **Pat Daly,** has edited each and every one of my books. There would be no Girl God Books without her enormous contributions. I was thrilled to also work again with one of my dearest sister-friends, **Tamara Albanna**—who took my daughter and I to see the Willendorf in person while we were visiting her in Vienna.

Tremendous gratitude to **Kat Shaw** for allowing us to use her inspired art on the cover—and contributing so many beautiful pieces of writing and art to this anthology.

Enormous appreciation to my husband **Anders Løberg**, who designed the cover, prepared the document for printing and helped with website updates. Your love, support and many contributions made this book possible.

My mom and I would also like to acknowledge her wonderful partner, **Rick Weiss,** for being an all-around awesome guy—and helping us with the page numbers and good cheer.

Lastly, I would like to thank my dear sister and fellow contributor **Alyscia Cunningham** for always being right there to cheer me on in the spirit of true sisterhood.

Thank you to all our readers and Girl God supporters over the years. We love and appreciate you!

Love and Blessings to all,
Trista Hendren

What's Next?!

Re-Membering with Goddess: Healing the Patriarchal Perpetuation of Trauma – Edited by Kay Louise Aldred, Trista Hendren and Pat Daly

Just as I Am: Hymns Affirming the Divine Female – **a Girl God Hermnal** – edited by Trista Hendren, Sharon Smith and Pat Daly

Wounded Feminine: Grieving with Goddess – Edited by Claire Dorey, Trista Hendren, and Pat Daly

Asherah: Roots of the Mother Tree – Edited by Claire Dorey, Janet Rudolph, Pat Daly and Trista Hendren

Sacred Breasts – Edited by Barbara O'Meara and Trista Hendren

The Wisdom of Cerridwen: Transforming in Her Cosmic Brew – Edited by Emma Clark, Trista Hendren, and Pat Daly

Lady of the Forge: Stories and Art Dedicated to the Goddess Brigid – Edited by Isca Johnson, Trista Hendren, and Pat Daly

Songs of Solstice: Goddess Carols – Edited by Trista Hendren, Sharon Smith and Pat Daly

Rainbow Goddess – Celebrating Neurodiversity – Edited by Kay Louise Aldred, Tamara Albanna, Trista Hendren and Pat Daly

Women's Sovereignty and Body Autonomy Beyond Roe v. Wade – Edited by Arlene Bailey, Pat Daly, Sharon Smith and Trista Hendren

Pain Perspectives: Finding Meaning in the Fire – Edited by Kay Louise Aldred, Trista Hendren and Pat Daly

For recent writings and news of upcoming publications, join us on Patreon @girlgodbooks!

If you enjoyed this book, please consider writing a brief review on StoryGraph, Amazon and/or Goodreads.